TRACING YOUR
VICTORIAN ANCESTORS
A GUIDE FOR FAMILY HISTORIANS

TRACING YOUR
VICTORIAN ANCESTORS
A GUIDE FOR FAMILY HISTORIANS

JONATHAN OATES

Pen & Sword
FAMILY HISTORY

First published in Great Britain in 2026 by
PEN AND SWORD FAMILY HISTORY
An imprint of
Pen & Sword Books Ltd
Yorkshire – Philadelphia

Print ISBN 978 1 03614 968 0
ePUB ISBN 978 1 03614 969 7
ePDF ISBN 978 1 03614 971 0

A CIP catalogue record for this book is available from the British Library

Typeset in 12/16 Palatino by SJmagic DESIGN SERVICES, India.
Printed and bound in the UK by CPI Group (UK) Ltd, Croydon, CR0 4YY.

The Publisher's authorised representative in the EU for product safety is Authorised Rep Compliance Ltd., Ground Floor, 71 Lower Baggot Street, Dublin D02 P593, Ireland.
www.arccompliance.com

For a complete list of Pen & Sword titles please contact

PEN & SWORD BOOKS LTD
George House, Units 12 & 13, Beevor Street, Off Pontefract Road,
Barnsley, South Yorkshire, S71 1HN, England
E-mail: enquiries@pen-and-sword.co.uk
Website: www.pen-and-sword.co.uk

or

PEN & SWORD BOOKS
1950 Lawrence Rd, Havertown, PA 19083, USA
E-mail: uspen-and-sword@casematepublishers.com
Website: www.penandswordbooks.com

MIX
Paper | Supporting responsible forestry
FSC® C013604

CONTENTS

ACKNOWLEDGEMENTS

I would like to express my thanks to Ruth Costello and John Gauss for having read through the book's chapters and thus avoiding the author expressing many errors throughout; any missed are entirely the author's own fault. Many of the pictures used here are from Paul Lang's collection, as always very kindly lent to the author. Some pictures were used by kind permission of Mrs Su Larson of Christ the Saviour School, Ealing, who also kindly let the author research through her school's Victorian archives. Ruth also supplied a picture.

This book is dedicated to my late mother-in-law, Mrs Mavis Bignell.

INTRODUCTION

The Victorian age of 1837–1901, which is named after the second longest reigning British monarch, is known for much. It can be a term of abuse or a term of respect. It is recalled in the novels of the Brontë sisters, Charles Dickens, Arthur Conan Doyle, Thomas Hardy, George Elliot and Antony Trollope, and in films such as *Zulu* and *The Charge of the Light Brigade*, or in the TV dramatisations of the novels of the writers of the era. It was an age of industry, improvement, democracy, education and Empire. Its monuments, such as the Victoria and Albert Museum, and numerous street names and pub names (even that used in a well known television soap opera) are still reminders of that era.

It was certainly a period of immense change for Britain; all eras are, of course, but perhaps more so here. At its beginning, though railways had been invented, there were relatively few; by its end the country was crisscrossed with an immense rail network and on the roads were electric trams and the first horseless carriages. At the beginning there was no photography but by the era's end, not only was it commonplace, but there were also telephones and moving pictures. Education became universal and far more of the increasingly literate newspaper-reading population could vote. More and more people lived in towns and cities than ever before as industrial employment overtook that on the land. The trade union movement was advancing and with it the Independent Labour Party. Although the British Empire was wider than ever, there were a number of rising powers to challenge it, despite general peace in Europe. There was increasing governmental intervention in society and religious practices became more diverse. The result was that more was recorded on paper and more of this was kept than in previous centuries.

For the family historian it is a critical era on at least two levels. First, 1837 marks not only the beginning of an era and a new monarch, but (for England and Wales) the beginning of centrally recorded civil registration of births, marriages and deaths; and second, 1841 saw the start of the national census, held every ten years, in which *everyone* was to be recorded, with age, address and occupation rather than just householders' names or household numbers as in previous censuses. From 1851 it became increasingly detailed. These are two of the most important, accessible and well used sources for family historians.

These records are important building blocks for identifying ancestors and for obtaining clues for the next steps to take in research. They should identify names, ages, occupations and places where ancestors lived as well as indicating other family members. This book assumes that the reader has already undertaken this research; if not then it should be done at the outset. Thus the imagined reader will already have a handful of names of ancestors with information about their locations and occupations and knowledge of their birth, marriage and deaths – or at least some of them.

Yet they are not the only ones and this book will introduce the reader to many more for this very important period of history. All of these archives are open to inspection, unlike the case for some twentieth-century records. The longest closure period (in the case of some medical and educational records as well as the census) is a century and so there is no problem with data protection laws here as there is with many of the twentieth century's archives. It was also a more literate, democratic and educated era and this led to an increase in the amount of written documents being created and being kept by institutions which are still with us.

Most books about family history are either general, or focus on a particular group, often by occupation, or are about a particular region or even city. This is one of the few books to attempt to cover a period of time. It will do so without attempting a history of the Victorian era, of which there are many books to hand. Nor will it try to provide an in-depth look at particular professions or social groups.

What it will do is alert the investigator as to what is available and where they should look, as well as research hints from an author who is both a custodian of archives and a researcher into them. Not all these sources will be useful and not all will exist for the person you are seeking. All historical research is a hunt which will lead to who knows where; some dead ends, but also some treasure troves too. Happy hunting and good luck.

Chapter 1

GENERAL ASPECTS OF VICTORIAN FAMILY HISTORY RESEARCH

Sources – originals and substitutes

The nineteenth century generated a great amount of paperwork, far more than had the previous century. This is due in part to a rising population, and in part to the growth of universal literacy. For the first time in history there were photographs and so the visual representation is far greater than in any time hitherto. Some of what was produced remains to be used by researchers, and that is a great quantity.

Of this material, some is only accessible to researchers in its original format. Others are not – parish registers, newspapers and census returns, for example, have only been visible on microfilm, and then electronically, for decades, except in rare circumstances. This is in order to preserve this unique material from overuse. Extremely valuable items, such as the papers relating to the Jack the Ripper murders, are only available in substitute format.

In recent decades repositories and commercial providers have focused on the digitisation of archives and these have prioritised sources for the family historian because of the topic's popularity and its financial viability. A great deal of research is now possible to do at the touch of keyboard buttons. The provision of payment sites such as FindMyPast, Ancestry and the British Newspaper Archive, are discussed more fully in Chapter 11 of this book.

Some archives have been transcribed (copied) onto paper format by county and other record societies and published. A number of Victorian era diaries (e.g., those of the Rev. Francis Kilvert of the 1870s) and letters have been commercially published. These have the advantage over the originals in that they are printed and so any problem with understanding manuscript handwriting has hopefully been resolved by the editor, and these works will also be indexed and so provide additional information about the events and individuals described therein which would be recorded in official documentation. Some diaries have been digitised and so can be searched online by keyword; the Royal Archives did so with Queen Victoria's diaries.

Kilvert often commented about people he met or knew of. In February 1874 he wrote of one Frank Vincent, 'the handsome young Dragoon … He is a noble young soldier and singularly attractive and lovable.' Not everyone was so complimented, for on the next day he wrote 'Greatly troubled by the licentiousness of the school children, especially Harriet Ferris, Mary Grimshaw and Lucy Halliday.' Vincent and Lucy are referred to again later that year by the diarist. These are unique insights into these people by one who knew them, though of course they are inevitably subjective.

The only issue here is that transcribers may not have made a complete copy of the original, they may have misspelt words or may have omitted parts of the original text. Many published versions of diaries and letters are only a fraction of the original and so the latter may well be worth investigating, and that is more difficult, because the manuscript is probably in a record office or library that has to be visited in person. Or in some cases the originals do not exist; as is the case with the complete Kilvert diaries, which were destroyed by a descendant and so now only the extracts published in three volumes can be read.

As for photographs, many have been digitised. Both Leeds and Manchester libraries have digitised all the photographs in their local history collections and so these can be seen for free online, and are searchable by keyword. The former is known as the LEODIS Image Archives, https:secretlibraryleeds.net/collections-reasures/collections/Leodis/ It is made up of 60,000 images drawn from a number of local repositories. Many other institutions have done, or are doing, the same with their visual collections. There are often photographs of groups of people, such as schoolchildren or footballers or others; archive repositories rarely have pictures of individuals unless they are particularly significant people such as a local mayor or vicar or someone of high social prominence.

The researcher must expect to view a mixture of originals and copies of material as part of their work. Both have their strengths and weaknesses; the former for completeness and the latter for accessibility and readability.

Family records and memorabilia: making contact with distant relatives

Immediate ancestors are usually easily known; most of us know the names and some details of our parents and grandparents, who may still be alive. But in the early twenty-first century there is no one alive who has experience of the Victorian era and very few have much personal recollection of the Second World War as the number of veterans sadly dwindles with time. So the Victorian era really is a foreign country which cannot be visited in person.

Family history is best started by immediate recourse to family members and especially those who have relevant

Daniel Howard, 1883. *(Author's family photograph)*

material. If you are lucky there might be photographs (hopefully with names and other details appended), letters or other personal documents. Many very ordinary people were photographed on a special occasion by a photographic studio, perhaps on the occasion of their marriage or on the birth of children, or even of a man going off to war.

Some prisons and asylums even sometimes photographed inmates. These documents might also include school or apprenticeship certificates or items associated with any clubs or societies they might have been involved with. There might be artefacts such as sports trophies or military medals. These are important clues as to where next to research. There may be family stories passed on orally about a particularly famous or infamous family member, or perhaps one who met a famous person or achieved some type of distinction. These stories lose nothing in the retelling but should be checked against contemporary sources. The ancestor who apparently won a VC at Rorke's Drift may turn out to be an infantryman who fought at Ulundi and was awarded a good conduct stripe. Not quite the same thing, but not without interest either. The embroidering of stories about ancestors is common – an ancestor being connected to a famous person is particularly common.

If no papers or artefacts survive it is certainly not the end of the world, genealogically speaking. But if they do exist they can be good starting points for further enquiry.

It is probably worth contacting distant relatives because it is possible that one of them might have worked on the family history. There is no point reinventing the wheel and going over old ground. Finding living relatives, if their names but not addresses are known, could be done by use of the online 192 searching device. Again, it is probably worth double checking anyone else's research results and examining what evidence was used to come up with them. A friend recently told me that he had got back to the fifteenth century using Ancestry alone by taking note of their 'suggestions'. This is not to decry the latter site at all, but to remind the researcher that every link in a chain of evidence needs testing to ensure it is valid. You need to be in position where you can say of your lineage, 'It is so long a chain and every link rings true' (*The Red Headed League*, Conan Doyle).

Selina Pryse and her father, c.1870s. *(Author's family photograph)*

Published pedigrees and family history

Some families in the nineteenth century and later had someone who was interested in their family history and wrote a book about that history, usually printed privately and in a very small print run as interest would inevitably be limited. Or there may be an autobiography. These may, or may not, have been published. If the former, these books may have been of a very limited number, published privately and chiefly aimed at distribution within the family only. Many of these were written by middle- and upper-class men or women who sought in part to glorify themselves and their families, rather than to write objective history, if indeed it is possible to write objectively about oneself and one's family. Although there are also memoirs of some trade unionists, working-class men, clergy and self-made men. Anything vaguely disreputable or dubious will be excised from these personal accounts, often by a son or other family member. On the other hand these accounts should not be discounted entirely, for the author may have had reference to family papers which now no longer exist.

The pedigree of Sir Edward Bowater was published in 1875 and was composed by one of the heralds of the College of Arms. These works were often part of a campaign to have the family granted a coat of arms.

There are a number of sources of listings of pedigrees. The British Biographical Archive is a compilation of 300 biographical dictionaries published between 1601 and 1929 and is arranged by surname. A copy can be seen at TNA (The National Archives) on microfiche and there is a printed index, The British Biographical Index, in the TNA library. Some pedigrees have been used to bolster legal claims and so can be found in TNA's legal records and so a search in Discovery using the term 'pedigree' and the family surname might yield useful results. As with all sources, pedigrees should be substantiated with other records but they can be a useful source of material that could be true.

The Society of Genealogists' Library has hundreds of pedigrees. These are listed on their website by alphabetical order of surname. A visit there would be needed to view them.

There are also opportunities online for contacting others who have the same research interests. FindMyPast has a family tree research facility to search for ancestors who are deceased and can be searched by typing in the name of the person sought and signing up for free. Ancestry has a similar facility. Finally, family history societies often publish lists of surnames that are being sought by other people.

Social status and social mobility

Eighteenth-century society was dominated by the nobility and gentry, but in the nineteenth century there was more of a place for new men who had made their money from trade and industry. Robert Peel, Prime Minister from 1841 to 1846, was from a background of business, as was Benjamin Disraeli, another prominent Victorian prime minister. Having said that, other prime ministers of the era were noblemen, such as the Earl of Derby, Viscounts Melbourne and Palmerston, Lord Russell and the Earl of Sailsbury. Charles Dickens was the son of a clerk who had been in a debtors' prison while his son became widely feted, and wealthy, for his novels. Men could rise to prominence in the armed forces or in working-class organisations.

On the other hand, many people remained in the same social class into which they were born. Others fell, socially and economically. Alcohol could cause the ruin of some once hardworking and respectable working men and women. The agricultural depression of the 1870s led to country estates being sold and some noblemen had to be propped up by marriages to wealthy American young ladies.

For those at the top of the social tree it may be worth consulting Debrett's *Peerage and baronetage* and Burke's *Peerage* and Burke's *Landed Gentry*. These were almost annual publications in the Victorian era. These should show who was who among the gentry and nobility and who was not there. However, some of the pre-Victorian genealogy has been condemned as being suspect by those such as the Victorian professor, John Round.

Some copies of Burke's can be seen on Ancestry. In the edition for 1881, information about the current nobleman is given, and also that of his siblings, children, father and lineage. We learn in this one that Sir Robert William-Colebrooke Brownrigg was born on 29 July 1819 and that he had been baronet since the death of his grandfather on 27 May 1833 (his father predeceased his grandfather). His armorial details are given, as are his club, The Travellers, and his London residence, 12 Eaton Place West.

The local area

It is a good idea for the family historian to have an understanding of the locality in which their ancestors lived. This will give context to their lives and will also suggest other record sources to explore. Most places have a published history about that town or village, so that might be the first place to look for a historical overview which hopefully will cover the Victorian era. Most will; it is often the later twentieth century and beyond which is skimped. There may be a bibliography to show you suggestions for further reading and source material. Most places will have books of old photographs devoted to a particular town and village and though many may be pictures from the Edwardian era and later, some may be older. A nineteenth-century map or maps would also be useful, as would a local directory (both these sources are discussed in more detail later in the book).

Mention has already been made of published diaries; few of our ancestors will have kept such personal documents and likewise correspondence or memoirs (though if you have one or can find them, they would be invaluable). However, if your research into the locality/localities in which your ancestors lived results in the discovery that someone else locally did so (usually someone of a high social standing with the leisure to do so), they may be worth a look. First, they should give an insight into the locality and its people and second, if you are really lucky they may refer to your ancestors, especially if they were in the same social circle or otherwise had some connection, not only geographical, with them.

Local history societies are often worth contacting because this is a way to tap the knowledge of people who are interested and knowledgeable about the history of a particular locality. A friend who is in the Surbiton Historical Society tells me that enquiries about houses and their former occupants are frequent, from people from all over the world.

Spelling names, names and naming patterns

The spelling of names was increasingly standardised throughout the century because more and more information was published and therefore printed. That being said, names were often spelt differently in different documents. Sharpe could be spelt Shairp or Sharp or Shairpe. Or alternative names might be used, or middle names as first names and so on. Often a father would give his first son his own name or the first daughter her mother's name. If the eldest son or daughter died in infancy then a later son/daughter might receive the same name as the deceased sibling.

Spelling is also an issue when names are being recorded by others who might mishear what is being said to them. Possibly the speaker has a different accent to the recorder (e.g., birth place Culmstock, Devon recorded in Yorkshire as Calmstock, because a Devonian doesn't pronounce it Coolmstock!); there is even the possibility that they might be inebriated or have missing teeth. Those giving the information to officials might be illiterate and so could not check the spelling of what was written down. They may not have known the correct spelling. Indeed, it is debatable as to what was 'correct'. Perhaps it is that it was only with the advent of universal – or near universal – primary education, that children would have been given a spelling of their name by their teacher and only then would it become frozen in their branch of the family. If information is being recopied then it is possible that errors might be perpetuated. If the first letter or two of a name is written down incorrectly then searching for that name can be difficult.

In 2024 I was searching for a name in the 1891 census; it was a young man born in 1874 and who died in 1929, but in 1891 was not recorded as living with his family in Yorkshire, nor at the boarding school where two of his brothers had attended. It was highly likely he was living in England and at a boarding school somewhere, but where? I decided to use the other information known about him – his Christian name, his place and year of birth – and see what a search in the census without a surname would bring. The search was successful and the reason why a surname search was not, was because the surname had been horribly mangled when written down. Or possibly, the first name has been badly written down and a surname based search might be needed. So the trick is to use what you do know and see what that brings up. It turned out that he was living with a relative, his mother's sister. That might have been another search technique; to search other branches of a family to see if a child might be living with them or if one sibling was living with another, as in the case of two of the Everard sisters in 1891.

Handwriting

Although the typewriter was being introduced at the end of the Victorian era (Sherlock Holmes notes that women office workers used such a device), for most of these decades writing was manuscript, especially for documents not intended for general consumption. These could include minute books, magistrates' records and much more. However, unlike some of the writing in the early eighteenth century and before, it will be in English. That does not necessarily mean it will be easy to read, as anyone who has looked at the census returns of 1841–1901 will readily testify. In 2025 I was showing a reader a vestry minute book covering 1860 and she said that she found it difficult to read.

Researchers will know from having seen census returns and civil registration documents that the quality of handwriting varies considerably, from the beautiful copperplate which is a pleasure, to read to illegible scrawl that would disgrace the proverbial doctor. Writing meant to be read by another, e.g., letters, should be more legible than writing in diaries not meant for general consumption. Having said that there was a tendency to write on both sides of a piece of paper and sometimes even diagonally, which does not aid reading these letters.

As with anything in life when one is first trying to do something it can be challenging, but as always practice and repetition help. It may be useful to take each word at a time and even each letter. With practice, reading nineteenth-century script will become easier and quicker. It is not always necessary to understand every word in a document as the meaning can often be understood without 100 per cent comprehension. If you are stuck over one word, move onto the next and maybe come back to the difficult one which may now be more legible because you have come across more recognisable words.

If you can copy the document electronically you can then pore over it at leisure rather than wasting valuable time at a record office. You could also ask a family member or friend to have a second look for you. It is not generally good form to ask record office staff to help with 'translation', but perhaps help might be rendered for the occasional word.

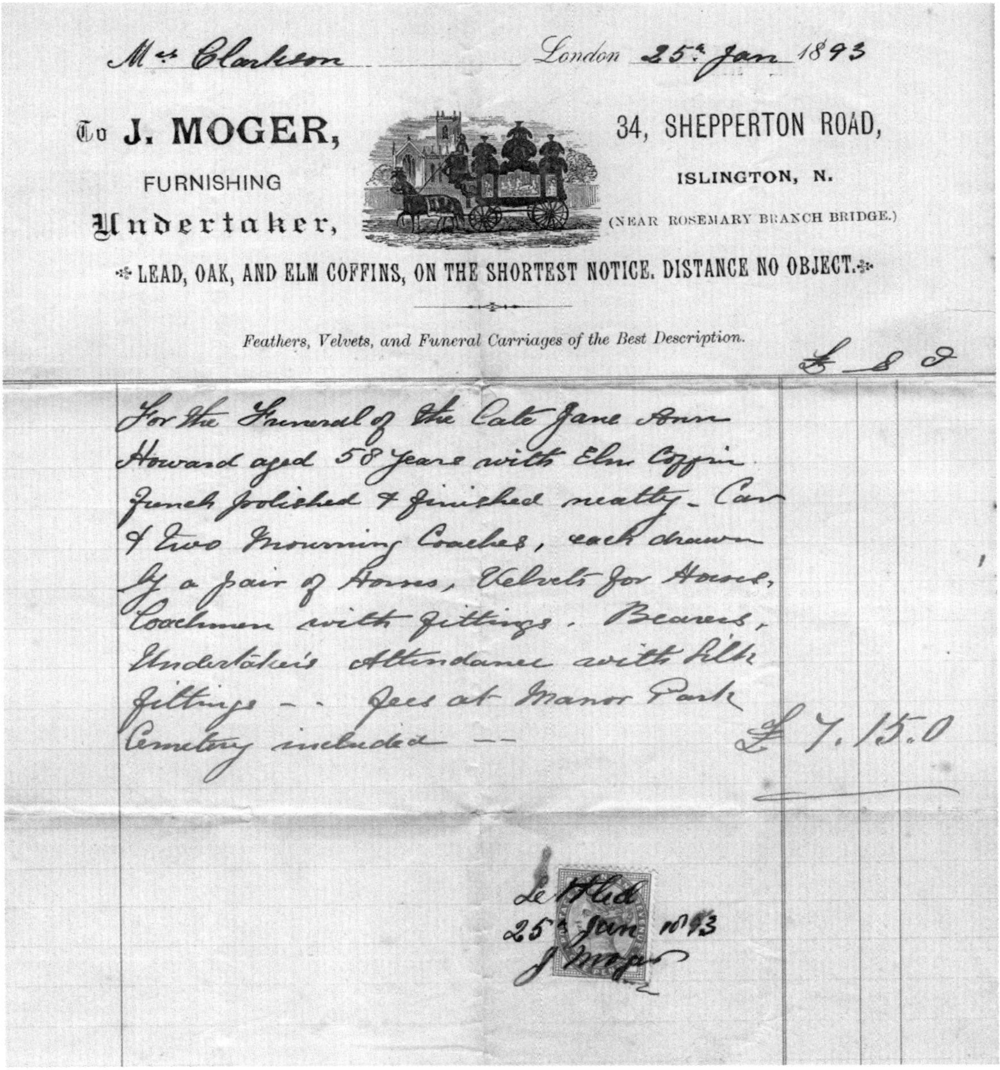

Mrs Clarkson London 25th Jan 1893

To J. MOGER, FURNISHING Undertaker,

34, SHEPPERTON ROAD, ISLINGTON, N. (NEAR ROSEMARY BRANCH BRIDGE.)

LEAD, OAK, AND ELM COFFINS, ON THE SHORTEST NOTICE. DISTANCE NO OBJECT.

Feathers, Velvets, and Funeral Carriages of the Best Description.

£ s d

For the Funeral of the Late Jane Ann Howard aged 58 years with Elm Coffin french polished & finished neatly - Car & two Mourning Coaches, each drawn by a pair of Horses, Velvets for Horses, Coachmen with fittings. Bearers, Undertaker's Attendance with Silk fittings -- Fees at Manor Park Cemetery included -- £7.15.0

Settled 25th Jan 1893 J Moger

Funeral expenses for Jane Howard, 1893. *(Author's family document)*

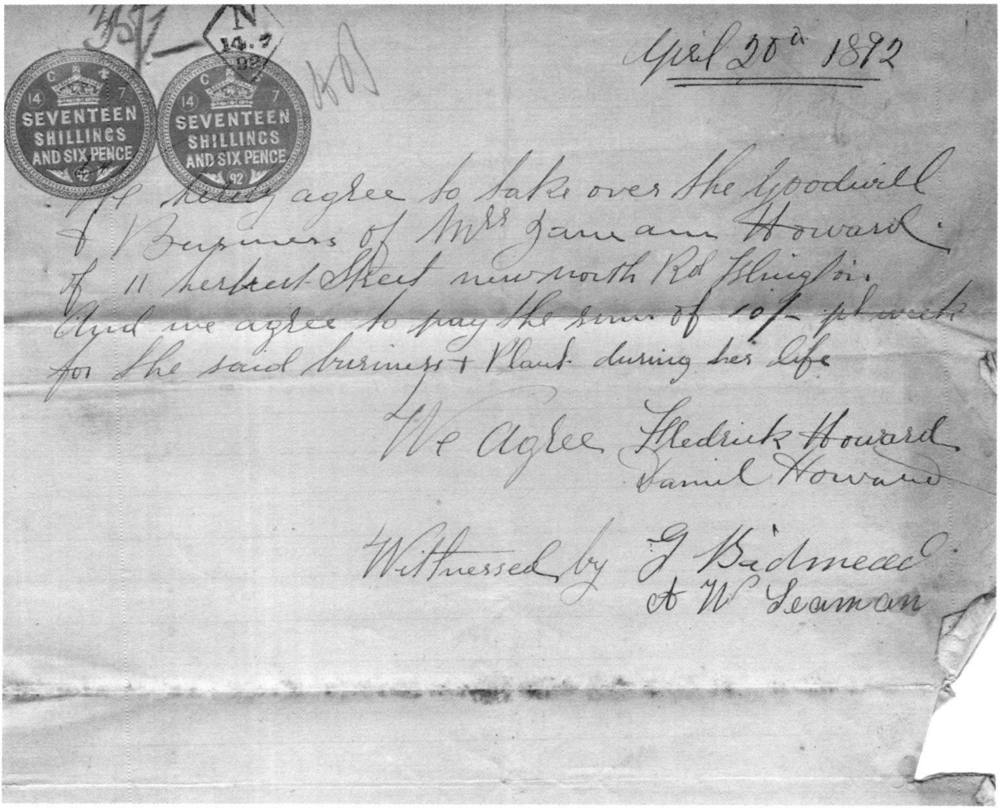

SEVENTEEN SHILLINGS AND SIX PENCE

SEVENTEEN SHILLINGS AND SIX PENCE

April 20th 1892

We hereby agree to take over the Goodwill & Business of Mrs Jane ann Howard of 11 Herbert Street new north Rd Islington. And we agree to pay the sum of 10/- per week for the said business & Plant during her life

We agree Frederick Howard
Daniel Howard

Witnessed by G Bidmead
A W Seaman

Agreement for takeover of Howard family business, 1892. *(Author's family document)*

Chapter 2

FURTHER SOURCES FOR LIFE EVENTS: BIRTHS, MARRIAGES AND DEATHS

Civil registration certificates and entries in parish registers record the births (and baptisms), marriages and deaths (and burials) of our ancestors. However, there are additional sources for these major mileposts in their lives. The growth of literacy through the expansion of schools in the early part of our period and then through compulsory elementary education after 1880 was important in creating a mass market for newspapers. More titles were established and more people read them. The abolition of tax on newspapers in 1855 and 1861 also meant that they could be produced more cheaply.

Newspaper announcements

There are two main types of family newspaper story. The first are the paid announcements. Those who could afford it often inserted announcements into the press to alert others to the occasion of births, marriages and deaths in their family. Newspapers had a regular column with such news. Yorkshire solicitor Harold Greenwood (1874–1929), then resident in London, paid to announce his marriage in 1896 and the birth of his first child two years later and these appeared in *The London Evening Standard*. His marriage was recorded thus:

> GREENWOOD-BOWATER, June 2nd, at All Saints, Edmonton, by the Reverend L. Hughes, M.A., Harold, second son of the late William Greenwood, Esq., of Greenwood Legh, Ingleton, Yorks. Mabel, younger daughter of William Vanstittart Bowater, of Bowater Hall, Edmonton, London N.

Then, with the birth of his first daughter:

> 3rd April 1898 – Greenwood, birth at Ingleton Bush Hill, Edmonton, a daughter.

It will be noted that at the birth no name had yet been assigned and the baptism may be some weeks away.

Deaths were also highlighted. For example, The *Middlesex County Times* for 18 October 1879 had the following death announcement:

> On the 11th of October, at 2, Bertha Villas, Avenue Road, Acton, Sarah Sophia, the beloved wife of George Wood in her 29th year.

Deaths abroad might be noted in these columns and there were sometimes 'In Memoriam' notices about a family member who had died some years ago but was still being remembered. All entries are usually brief. Marriages and deaths are often noted in greater detail elsewhere; an obituary of a prominent resident will give more biographical information, and a report of the funeral often lists the most significant mourners, and that of a wedding usually records guests and sometimes even the presents given.

It is worth noting that our Victorian ancestors did not just inhabit some or all of the years 1837–1901, just as Shakespeare's plays were performed in the reigns of both Elizabeth I and James I, or of more relevance, the majority of the Sherlock Holmes stories by Conan Doyle were written after the queen's death (though almost all were set in her lifetime). Some of our Victorian ancestors will have died after 1901, but if suitably eminent, either locally or nationally, their obituaries will cover their Victorian years. So when octogenarian Charles Jones died in 1913 after having been Ealing's surveyor since 1863, much of his working life had been in the Victorian era and so would be useful in providing clues to his nineteenth-century life and career. However, be careful when using obituaries because they were often written with information by younger family members who would have no first-hand knowledge of their parents' early lives. So in the 1913 Jones obituary the reader is told that he was born in Norfolk (and this has been repeated in two local history books); but the 1851 census clearly shows that it was Surrey.

Birthplaces may also change drastically in different census returns. The householder might not know where the person was born, especially if they are not a member of his family (e.g., lodger, servant and so forth) or the enumerator may have written a ditto, or the individual might have mentioned the place they lived in when very young but had not been born there. Checking birth certificates and parish registers may resolve this issue.

Bastardy records

The issue of the poor was and is a perennial one for all concerned. With rising costs to the poor law and thus increased rates for the ratepayers, savings were sought wherever possible.

One of the issues was births outside wedlock. These automatically brought a cost to the ratepayers because money was needed for the birth of the infant (paying for a midwife) and for years of money to support mother and child until they could fend for themselves. This was an issue that was given to the magistrates to solve and one way of doing this was summoning the unwed mothers and mothers-to-be in order to ascertain who the father was and then ordering them to pay the costs involved. An Act of 1844, replacing the provisions of the 1834 New Poor Law, stated that the pregnant or new mother could apply to the magistrates for relief, who would then seek out the alleged father and assess whether he was indeed the father and oblige him to pay up.

An example from the Wimborne, Dorset, petty sessions of November 1849 is as follows. Ann Amey, on 22 November, was to be paid by John Smith weekly from 3 November 1*s* 3*d* and to be given 15*s* in cash. However, Jane Allen's claim against a man whose name is not recorded, was refused. Why these different decisions were made is unknown. One might speculate that Ann had a previously good character and that Smith was a known rogue, whereas perhaps the perceived moral standards of Jane were low and the man who she alleged was the father was a man of 'good character'.

Records are held with the quarter session papers in county record offices; some records can be searched on Ancestry; those for Wiltshire are on FindMyPast (1844–1914). In Scotland the mother was known as the Pursuer and the alleged father as the Defender. Paternity decrees from 1750 to 1922 in Scotland can be found on FindMyPast. These give information about the parties involved. In one instance, John Graham, a traveller in pianofortes and a piano tuner employed by Wood and Co., piano sellers, and resident of Waterloo Place, Edinburgh, was brought before the court on 16 July 1847. He was alleged to have made Ann Ronald, who was daughter of William Ronald, a mason of Ayr, pregnant and she had given birth to a girl on 24 November 1845.

Adoption and foundlings

There was no legal adoption until 1927, but families often took in the children of relatives whose parents were deceased. No paperwork would have been completed and in the absence of a paper trail, where the child was living can only be inferred from the census. Some charities, such as Barnardo's, arranged adoptions so there may be relevant information there. Dr Thomas Barnardo began his famous children's homes in east London in 1867 and the archives are held at the University of Liverpool.

In 1741 Thomas Coram founded the Foundlings Hospital in London and that continued until 1948. Mothers would deposit babies that they could not care for here and some survived but others did not. Archives for these children, which include petitions from parents for their child to be sent here and apprenticeship registers, can be found at The London Archives (TLA). The foundation still exists so a direct approach can also be made there.

Sometimes informal adoptions took place and other members of the family would take in an illegitimate child and pass them off as their own where officialdom was concerned.

Marriage records: overlap with civil registration

Although civil registration of marriages began in 1837 in England and Wales, Scotland in 1855 (see www.Scotlandspeople.gov.uk) and Ireland in 1864, it does not follow that every birth went recorded by the civil authorities and thus a birth certificate for all was not guaranteed (marriages and deaths almost always were as these were public ceremonies). Indeed, for several decades there was no penalty for not doing so. Even afterwards many families did

Marriage as shown in short story in *The Strand*, 1893. *(Author's copy of* The Strand, *1893)*

not have their children baptised or births registered. Mary Jane Kelly was murdered in 1888 but despite her boyfriend later telling what she had told him about her past in Ireland and Wales her birth record has never been found.

As time goes on civil registration became more and more accepted – and fines for non-compliance from 1875 doubtless helped the process. So, for some time after 1837 church registers still have an essential part to play in family history, though perhaps less so as the decades progress. However, transcriptions and indexing of baptism registers from 1837 is more limited than prior to civil registration so it is possible that some baptism registers have been overlooked.

Information on these certificates and on the indexes to them varies over time. For England and Wales, age at death appears on the indexes, mothers' maiden names appear on the birth indexes for our period and spouse's name appears on the marriage indexes respectively.

Although Scottish certificates appeared later than those for England and Wales, they do record more information. This includes the time of birth and the date and place of the parents' marriage on birth certificates. For marriages, the maiden names of the mothers of the two parties are often stated. In death certificates there is the marital status of the deceased, the name of their spouse, if married, and the names of their parents – and the profession of the father and maiden name of the mother. However, the names of parents are not always given and are sometimes incorrect depending on the knowledge available to the registrar, so do be careful.

Marriage settlements were common in the eighteenth century among propertied families. They continued in the Victorian era though became less necessary after the Married Women's Property Act of 1882. These arrangements were legal agreements in which trustees were appointed by the family of the bride in which they would bequeath her property or money to yield an income for her and any children but preventing the husband from touching the capital. A search on TNA's Discovery under the names of the parties being married should find this.

Up to 1858 divorce was very rare and only available by Act of Parliament; 318 are recorded. Readers may recall the issue that Mr Rochester faced in *Jane Eyre*. Even after that, divorce was very rare and difficult as well as scandalous. Charles Stewart Parnell, a well known Irish politician, caused controversy for his involvement with Mrs O'Shea, whom her husband divorced in 1890. Archives of divorce cases from 1858 to 1938 can be found at TNA (series J77), though are incomplete – especially as time goes by – as well as featuring in the press. Divorce was very rare among the majority of the population in the nineteenth century; separation was more common. Ancestry has images of divorce records from 1858 to 1918.

Britons who were born, married or died overseas, or even at sea, can be found in a number of sources. These can be searched online and are as follows: Miscellaneous Foreign Returns, 1831–1969 (RG32); Foreign Registers and Returns, 1627–1960 (RG33); Miscellaneous Death Returns, Certificates and Death Registers, 1791–1921 (RG35); and Registers and Returns of Births, Marriages and Deaths in Africa and Asia, 1895–1965 (RG36). BT159 are registers of deaths at sea from 1874 to 1888 and can be searched, and BT 334 covers registers of births, marriages and deaths of passengers and seamen from 1891 to 1972, giving name, age, rank, birthplace and land address, and can be seen on FindMyPast.

Burial records

Apart from entries in parish registers and death certificates, the other prime record of death is burial, which is usually some days after death and in urban districts was usually in cemeteries. In the Victorian era churchyards in cities and towns gradually became full and there were concerns about the implications of this for public health. In the countryside the solution was to buy more land to adjoin the existing churchyard. Elsewhere, cemeteries were established and run by a number of officials in a burial board as an adjunct to either a parish and later a council. Some were run by private companies, such as the London Cemetery Company, which created Highgate Cemetery in 1839. They would buy land, often in the countryside, establish a chapel or usually two, one for Anglican ceremonies and one for nonconformist ceremonies.

Grave registers would be created to list who was buried where and when. Often, a family would buy a plot in order to enable future family members to be buried there with their loved ones. The registers are often located at the cemetery office itself but some may have been deposited at a county or borough record office, especially if that cemetery has been closed for new graves, in which case they should be with the parish records. Usually cemetery offices can be visited when the cemetery is open and staff consulted without an appointment; Brighton's is an example, but some cemeteries do not have an office on site, such as Plumstead in south east London. It is therefore worth checking availability prior to any visit.

Cemetery records will also give the plot number where a burial took place and so this, together with the aid of a plan of the cemetery, should help you to locate your ancestor's burial plot. Some memorials and graves can be searched online at Findagrave. An example in the Acton grave register is of plot A27, of Katie Priscilla Harrington, interred on 23 April 1893. Some have several names and have the name of the purchaser and the date.

It should also be remembered that even though a grave plot has been located and a plot reference found, there may be no actual gravestone. Gravestones cost money to install and maintain and many of our ancestors will have no such memorial. Even those that do exist are often faded and worn and so it may not be possible to read the wording. As a rule, the richer the family, the more ornate cemetery monument will be there. See below for more details on this topic.

If you are lucky, funeral cards issued at the time by the family may still exist and they often give basic details of the

Mourning Card. *(Paul Lang's collection)*

funeral. Or the undertaker may still be in business and may have archives of their business going back to the nineteenth century.

Deaths of members of particular professions are easier to find by others if the person in question was a member of a professional body. So the *Pharmaceutical Journal* established in 1841 carried obituaries of pharmacists, and the *Globe and Laurel* covered Royal Marines. Those dying in coal mine disasters from 1600 can be searched in the database in the Coal Mining History Resource Centre, at http://www.cmhrc.co.uk.

Coroner's records

The office of coroner dates to 1194 and is usually held by a solicitor or doctor. They are called in on the occasion of any death which is unexpected. Readers of detective stories will know of these as they usually play a role in such narratives.

However, the bulk of inquests are held on accidental deaths and less frequently suicides; even less common are murders and manslaughters. Their job is to hear the evidence given by doctors, police and other witnesses to ascertain how and why someone died – in the event of murder the jury could even point the finger at their foremost suspect, who could then be arrested.

Archives relating to inquests are mostly held at county record offices (up to 1860 they should be filed in the quarter sessions records), but the majority do not survive. Where they do, the amount of information is variable. It is rare that it will be a verbatim account of the proceedings with full statements of witnesses and officials. In some cases inquests are catalogued by subject of the inquest, but not always. The inquest on John Smith, a child who was severely burnt in Brighton in 1846, comes up on a search at the East Sussex Record Office website, but the files on inquests elsewhere do not and so you would need to know when the inquest occurred and order the necessary file.

The only coroners' records on Ancestry are those for the West Riding of Yorkshire coroner from 1852 to 1909. It provides notes of all the inquests in the district at the time. For example, there was an inquest at William Smith's Welcome Inn at Alverthorpe on 22 March 1898. Martha Ogden of 14 Cross Lane, Boroughhouses, Alverthorpe, gave evidence about the recent demise of her husband, the 67-year-old John. He had been a gardener and died suddenly on his bed. Another witness had seen him walking along shortly beforehand and deemed him in good health. The inquest found that this was a case of death by natural causes. There are also some coroner's records on FindMyPast; those for Wiltshire from 1840 to 1901 also give detailed accounts of proceedings for that county.

Inquests are usually reported in the local press, however, and it could be said that although these were tragedies for the families at the time, they are a goldmine for family historians. A workman who dies peacefully in bed will rarely be mentioned in the press, but one who is killed by falling off a building at work will be news and so will garner attention, meaning you will learn more about his death, his life and his family.

An example of an inquest reported in *The Acton Gazette* for 15 August 1891 was as follows:

> **THE SUICIDE OF A LADY**
>
> The adjourned enquiry, touching the death of Mary Grant, of 1, Park-road North, was resumed on Saturday at the Mill Hill Park Hotel, by Dr. Diplock, the coroner. Mr Clifton was the foreman of the jury, and the following additional evidence was taken.
>
> Daisy Jarrett, of 7, Mill Hill-terrace, said she assisted in the housework at No.1, Park-road North. She was there on Wednesday morning, but did not see the deceased. She did not know whether deceased had her breakfast. She never used to see deceased. Witness left at ten o'clock and she told Mrs Eade she was leaving. Mrs Eade prepared the breakfast and she (Mrs Eade) breakfasted downstairs. She could not say whether or no Mrs Eade had breakfast with Miss Grant.
>
> In answer to question witness said she went to the house at 9 o'clock. She was not minding Mr Miller's house while he was in the country. A Mrs Gordon used to visit Miss Grant and she lived next door to the deceased.
>
> Dr Lingham, of Acton, said he had attended the deceased for 20 years. He called on Wednesday, when she was lying on a bed dead with a cord round her throat. The cord had made decided marks round the neck of strangulation, but of course it was loosely bound when he observed it. He had not made a post mortem

examination. His opinion was that strangulation was the cause of death. Deceased had had several shocks of late which undoubtedly contributed to making her of unsound mind. All the time he had been attending her she had been suffering from nervous depressions and the last time he saw her it was from inability to speak except in whispers.

In answer to questions, witness said it was not a case of hanging – it was strangulation. Deceased was most decidedly strong enough to strangle herself.

Dr Lingham said that an aunt of the deceased's had had her mind unhinged.

A juryman wished to ask Mrs Eade a few questions, and in response that lady said the cord produced was the one round the deceased's neck. She did not know where the deceased got it from. Deceased had a little money in the house: she would think about £25. She had only known that since the death. Deceased had a watch and chain and other trinkets, and to the best of her belief, they were all safe now.

The jury returned a verdict that deceased committed suicide, while of unsound mind, by strangulation.

One of the jurymen did not agree to the verdict, he being understood to be in favour of returning an open verdict. The verdict having been returned this gentleman proceeded to leave the court, but in reply to Mr Scales, the coroner's officer, Dr Diplock stated that the court had not yet been discharged, the juror accordingly resumed his seat with apologies to the coroner.

Memorial inscriptions and gravestones

Since the late Middle Ages churches and cathedrals included plaques to those associated with that church, though not necessarily buried there. These were almost always for the well-to-do whose families could afford to pay for a memorial to their family member; perhaps a beloved wife or a son who had died in battle or from disease overseas. This continued in the Victorian era. It was often in addition to gravestones in the churchyard or cemetery. There are inscriptions to Sir Spencer Walpole inside St Mary's parish church in Ealing and a gravestone to him in the cemetery half a mile away. Some memorials and gravestones may commemorate more than one person or there may be a cluster of plaques together in the same church if a particular family was prominent in that locality for some time, like as the Christie family of Hoddesdon, Hertfordshire, who are commemorated in St Augustine's church at Broxbourne.

Memorial inscriptions will give dates of birth and death, details of a man's career and achievements; a short eulogy in fact. An inscription for a woman will stress the virtues of her personality: usually fidelity and generosity. They may be short or lengthy; other family members may be referred to, with dates of death and ages on death. These can be likened to the eulogies at a funeral and naturally avoid anything detrimental to the deceased, so the researcher should not take them at face value.

One point about gravestones is that they often give family members' names who might not otherwise be known to the researcher. These include, for example, children who were born and died between the census years. Infant mortality was still at a high rate in some cases in the nineteenth century, despite advances in medicine. For instance, the Hall gravestone in the churchyard of St Peter's Iver reveals the name of a child, Caroline Jane Hall, who was born in December 1861 and died in September 1862.

Some memorial (or monumental) inscriptions can be searched for on Ancestry; including some for Scotland from 1507 to 2019 and for Northern Ireland inscriptions from 1658 to 2018. There are a number of English counties for which these are covered on FindMyPast: Northamptonshire, Suffolk, Cheshire, Wiltshire and Cornwall. Otherwise, the appropriate county record office or family history society for the district could be contacted. This is because many of the latter have compiled listings of these inscriptions both inside and outside churches. These are often indexed and are particularly valuable because some of the outdoor inscriptions may have faded away over time. The Society of Genealogists' Library also has a substantial collection.

Monumental inscriptions to some Britons who died abroad can be found in the British Library on shelves V27/74 in the monuments and inscriptions sections. British burials in India can be seen at http://indian-cemeteries.org and www.bacsa.org.uk. Others are at the Families in British Indian Society website, https://www.fibis.org, which has a list of cemeteries, and names of those buried there can be searched online. For example, at the old Christian cemetery at Abbottabad there are eighty-seven people listed; one being Constance Christina Davies, aged 11 years and six months, who died in 1860 and was the daughter of Lieutenant Colonel H.L. Bernard of the First Bengal European Regiment.

Memorial inscriptions can be found in churches other than where the ancestor lived. They may also be in a place with which they were associated, perhaps by being an absentee landowner for example; it is possible that such a plaque or plaques might be in more than one place, so it is worth checking.

There are other memorial boards in churches in addition to those for the deceased. There are boards listing the incumbents with their years of service, and boards listing charities and works in connection with the church. All these will be found in the main body of the church building. There are often boards to be found in the church bell tower, usually only accessible when bell ringing takes place (practice evenings and on Sundays). When the bell ringers perform

Memorial in All Saints church, Hastings. *(Author's photograph, 2025)*

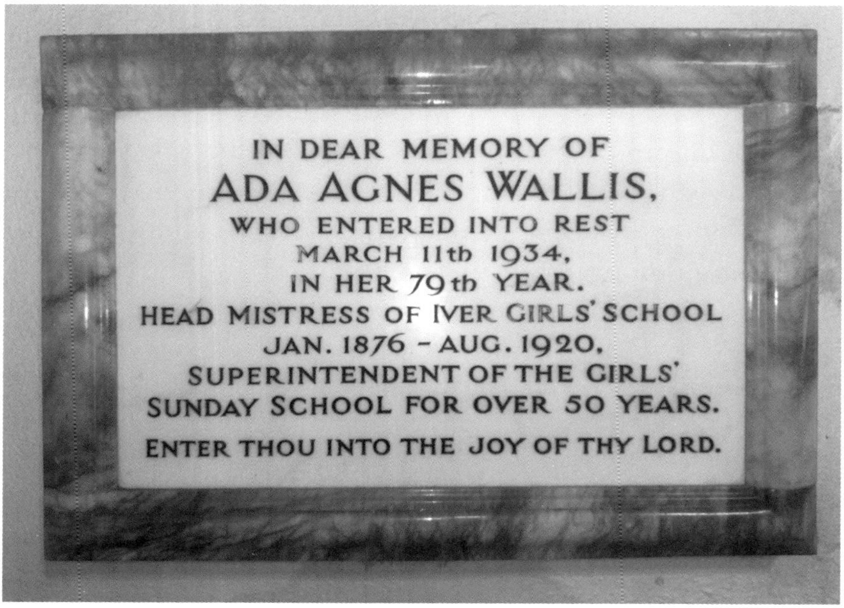

Memorial in St. Peter's church, Iver. *(Author's photograph, 2025)*

Churchyard at Cross Hills, Yorkshire. *(Author's photograph, 2025)*

an act of ringing, often a peal for three hours, perhaps to commemorate a notable event, such as a coronation, this is sometimes recorded and the list of the bell ringers is commemorated with the date and the event.

Wills

Until 1858 wills were administered by a bewilderingly diverse number of church courts, as had been the case since the Middle Ages. Many wills were dealt with by the archdeaconry courts if the testator's property fell in that archdeaconry. If they owned property in more than one archdeaconry but in the same diocese, then it was the bishop's consistory court that would administer it. If in more than one diocese then it was the archepiscopal court; so for the southern counties and the Midlands this was the Prerogative Court of Canterbury (PCC), and those in the north of England by the Prerogative Court of York (wills at the Borthwick Institute). If property was in both provinces the senior court (PCC) would deal with it. PCC wills can be searched at TNA and images of these wills can be viewed. But there were also a number of 'peculiar' courts whose jurisdiction was outside the archdeaconry court and often ran to a very small number of parishes. The wills proved by these are usually located at the diocesan record office.

Wills proved in Wales from 1544 to 1858 can be read for free on http://www.library.wales/ at top right click catalogue, then Advanced Search, then wills, and wills for a number of English counties can be found at FindMyPast, as well as servicemen's wills (army, 1850–1986 and navy and marines, 1786–1882).

From 1858 all wills in England and Wales were administered centrally and this makes matters easy for the family historian because they can all be searched for in one place. Wills.gov.uk is the main gateway for wills proved from 1858 onwards and this is discussed in Chapter 11. The importance of wills, which are generally, though not always, left by the middle and upper classes, is that they list other family members who are beneficiaries of the said will; with amounts to be given to them or perhaps property. It does not mean that is what they actually received as wills might have been made years before death and perhaps then the funds available to the testator had changed. Death duties, noted at this chapter's end, should be checked.

Dying intestate, not having a will, meant that the appropriate court would deal with a person's property. These were called Administrations, or Admons for short. This usually meant that the property went to the next of kin, but debtors could also be paid off with the estate. These can

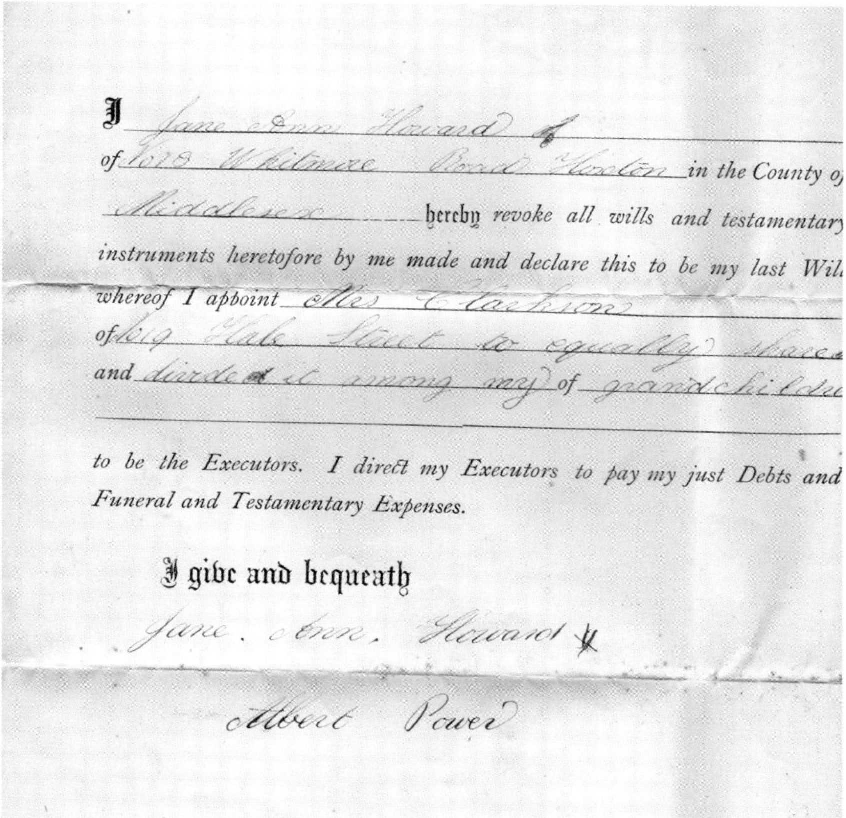

I Jane Ann Howard of

of [illegible] Whitmore Road Hoxton in the County of

Middlesex hereby revoke all wills and testamentary

instruments heretofore by me made and declare this to be my last Will

whereof I appoint Mrs Clarkson

of 19 Hale Street to equally share

and divide it among my of grandchildren

to be the Executors. I direct my Executors to pay my just Debts and Funeral and Testamentary Expenses.

I give and bequeath

Jane Ann Howard

Albert Power

Will of Jane Howard, 1893. *(Author's family document)*

also be found on the same site as mentioned in the previous paragraph.

Remember that until the Married Women's Property Act of 1882 on marriage all of a woman's estate would pass to her husband. Married women could not make wills, though marriage settlements often could counter this by only allowing a husband income from the wife's marriage portion during her lifetime without touching the capital. However, widows and spinsters could make wills just as men. Many people still did not leave wills, and will makers were still in a minority in this period – though an increasingly large one.

Scottish wills from 1514 to 1925 have been digitised and can be seen in Scotlandspeople Centre and in the National Records of Scotland in the Historic Search Room and on the Scotlandspeople website. They were proved in the sheriffs' courts from 1824 onwards. Most Irish wills prior to 1922 were destroyed in that year but any which relate to land elsewhere in Britain should survive in the source mentioned in the paragraphs above. There are also some surviving abstracts of wills.

Some wills can be very short and some very long. The will of Norman Greenwood of Ingleton, Yorkshire, was made in 1872, shortly after his marriage but before any children had been born. After listing set sums for his wife and mother, the residue of the estate, which was valued at under £18,000 in 1877, was to be equally divided between any the children of the marriage (there were four sons living at the time of his death). Before reaching the age of 21 the income from these portions was to be administered by the executors: their mother, Mrs Isabella Greenwood, and James Henry Vant, a solicitor of Whitefriars, Settle, for the maintenance and education of the boys. On attaining the age of 21 the capital sums were to be given to the four sons.

Wills may list bequests to servants and to friends and may refer to cash sums or particular pieces of property, which helps to flesh out a little of their life as to whom they thought highly of. Or they might just state that everything goes to the testator's spouse.

Wills are occasionally mentioned in the press if there is some particularly unusual feature or there was a large sum involved. There are also death duty registers at TNA, where an estate was investigated for tax purposes. These cover 1796–1903 for estates worth over £1,500 and are a useful addition to wills. IR26 is the series of registers with an index in IR27 which is needed to be used to find what you are looking for in the series of registers. They provide details of a testator's estate at the time of death, which may not be the same as the provisions of a will which was often made years previously when the financial circumstances of the testator may have been different. Some of these prior to 1858 can be searched for and seen online but not those after 1858, though the indexes can be searched for on FindMyPast.

Chapter 3

EDUCATION AND EMPLOYMENT

Much of our ancestors' lives were taken up by their daytime activities, and indeed working hours were far longer than they were to become in the later twentieth century. Paid holidays were the exception, not the norm.

School and university records

The Victorian era saw an unprecedented increase in those attending educational institutions. Schools were established by both the Anglican Church and by the nonconformist chapels in the early to mid-nineteenth centuries. This was especially the case after 1833 with the introduction of government subsidies. The former were known as National Schools and the latter as British Schools, and though the religious part of the curriculum was denominational, the pupil intake was not. By 1851 these schools numbered 17,000 and 1,500 respectively. Other early schools were the ragged schools from 1844 (there were 200 by 1869) and the more vocational industrial schools. Log books and admission registers from some of the National Schools from 1870 to 1914 can be searched on FindMyPast; they give the name of the school and the dates of attendance, with the pupil's address.

St. Mark's School, Hanwell. *(Author's photograph, 2025)*

The 1870 Forster Education Act allowed local government in England and Wales to provide for schools where existing church and charity school provision was insufficient. School Boards were established to build and maintain them. Often the words 'Board School' can still be seen on the exterior of older school buildings which are still in use. Schooling was only compulsory in 1880 and then to the age of 10; in 1893 and 1899 the leaving age was raised first to 11 then to 12. All elementary schooling was free from 1891; previously a small fee was required.

Higher education also increased; the university of London expanded its colleges and other universities were established such as those in Durham, Liverpool and Manchester. Oxford and Cambridge colleges increased in number. Aberystwyth university college was founded in 1872 and Cardiff a decade later.

As far as we are concerned, the main series of records created by schools were registers of pupils attending them. They list, in chronological order, names of pupils entering by autumn term, with date of birth, date of entry, father's name and address and date of departure and reason for that. This might state the school to which they moved, or employment on leaving. Their previous school might also be noted.

An example from the admission register of Christ Church School, Ealing, is of John Stacey of East Cottage, Broadway. He was born on 28 June 1881 and entered the school on 8 October 1888. He had previously been to school in Finsbury Park and left the Ealing school on 24 June 1892.

However, not all registers survive and this is certainly the case with many of the earlier years of some schools. Furthermore, of the many small private schools which once existed, most archives ceased to exist when the school folded.

There are other school archives. Punishment books can be a useful source for the minority of recalcitrant pupils, arranged in chronological order. These list the name of the pupil, the number of strokes of the cane awarded, the reason for the caning the date and the name of the administrator.

We should note that school records also have information about staff, and often more so than those for pupils. One other key source are school log books and these survive in greater quantity than school registers. They were composed by the school's head about events occurring at the school. These can refer to events such as a visit by the school inspectors, sports days, the beginning and end of terms and so on. Pupils are mentioned only very rarely. Rather it is the teachers who are mentioned more often; lists of staff are given. When a staff member is absent due to illness or family reasons, they are usually noted, when a new staff member is appointed or leaves they will be recorded. Log books are not indexed and few if any are available online, but if you know that an ancestor worked in or attended a school, then the log books, if they exist, should be read.

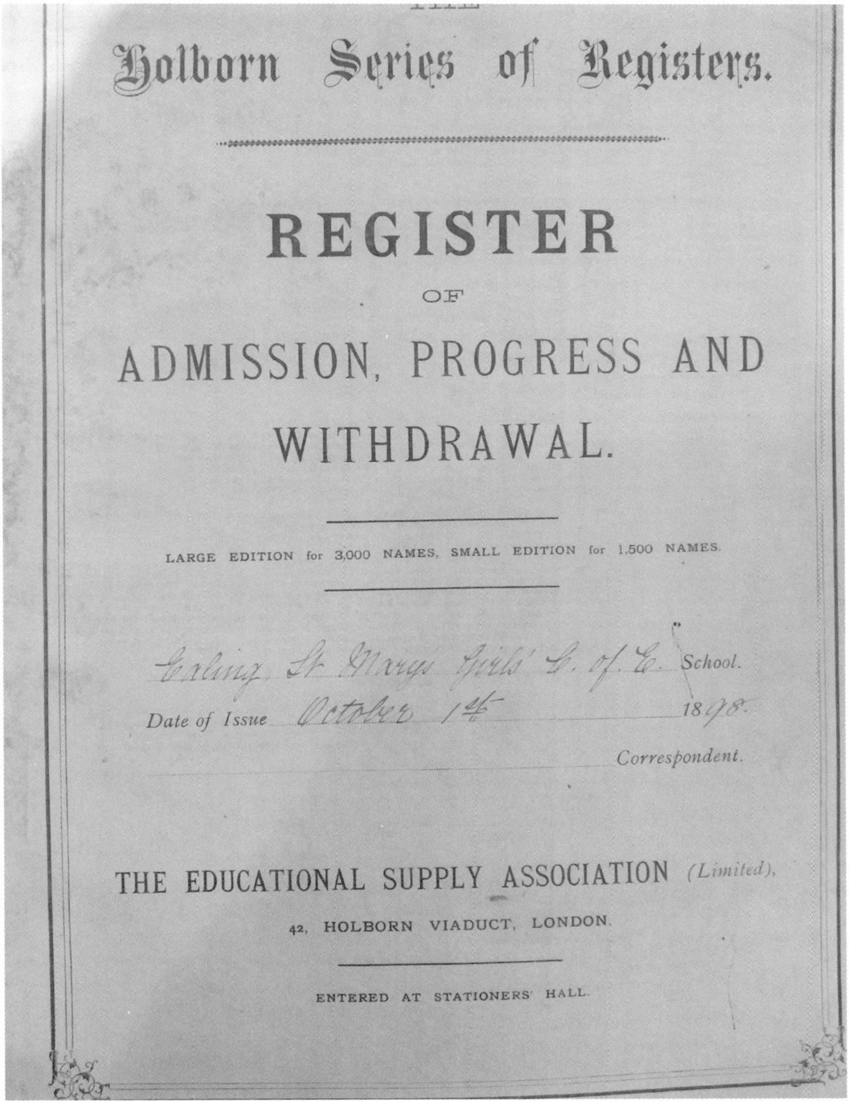
Holborn Series of Registers.

REGISTER

OF

ADMISSION, PROGRESS AND

WITHDRAWAL.

LARGE EDITION for 3,000 NAMES, SMALL EDITION for 1,500 NAMES.

Ealing, St Marys Girls' C. of E. School.

Date of Issue October 1st 1898.

Correspondent.

THE EDUCATIONAL SUPPLY ASSOCIATION (Limited),

42, HOLBORN VIADUCT, LONDON.

ENTERED AT STATIONERS' HALL.

School Register of pupils, St. Mary's School, Ealing. *(Christ the Saviour School, Ealing)*

The log book of the National School of the rural parish of Northolt, Middlesex, does occasionally mention pupils by names, mainly for the wrong reasons, though this gives an insight into country life at the time. On 15 May 1882 it was noted, 'Henry Saunders and Henry Rose still absent from

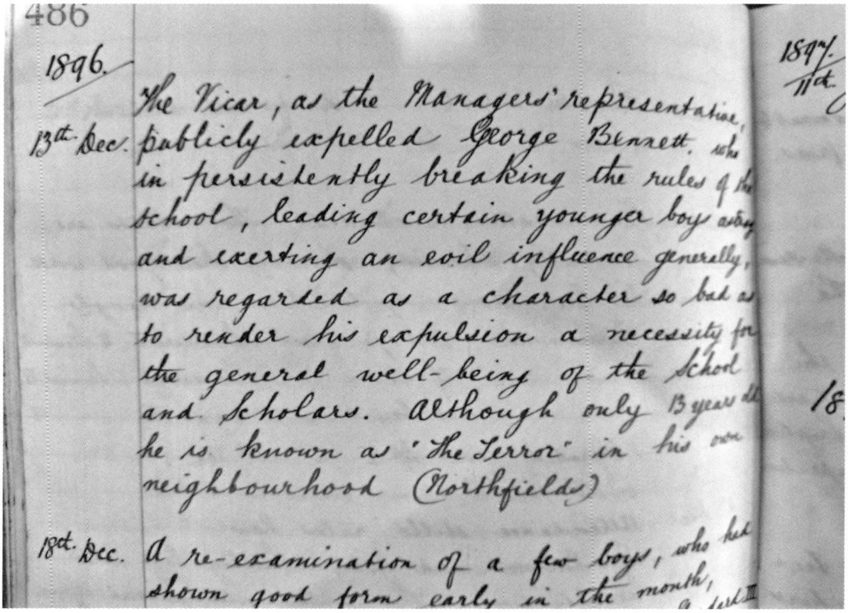
486

1896.

13th Dec. The Vicar, as the Managers' representative, publicly expelled George Bennett, who in persistently breaking the rules of the school, leading certain younger boys astray and exerting an evil influence generally, was regarded as a character so bad as to render his expulsion a necessity for the general well-being of the School and Scholars. Although only 13 years old he is known as 'The Terror' in his own neighbourhood (Northfield)

18th Dec. A re-examination of a few boys, who had shown good form early in the month,

Log book page of Christ Church school, Ealing. *(Christ the Saviour School, Ealing)*

school for work in the brickfields.' Later that year, 'Eliza Reynolds absent all week with her brother working in the hay fields.' More bizarrely, on 9 February 1886, 'William Anstead remained outside in the road all day and I asked two boys to bring him in but he refused. On 10th he received two strokes.' Or, even odder, in the case of Christ Church school in Ealing, on 28 August 1874, 'E. Coomes brought a quantity of gunpowder to school, quite loose, in his pocket. He was warned of the danger, and a notice sent to his parents by J. Coutts.'

It was not only the disobedient mentioned in these log books. At the latter school there are the following references in the log book:

18 September 1874: 'H. Baker absent through want of trousers.'

21 March 1879: 'W. Freebrey was withdrawn from school this week, the reason given for his withdrawal being that

he might go to a school where his little brother could be received also, the latter was too young to be admitted here.'

27 September 1895: 'Chas. Frost and Joseph Hartley of Northfields are kept from school by order of the doctor on account of an outbreak of diphtheria in their houses.'

Most existing school records are held at the appropriate county or borough archives. However, some schools still retain their Victorian era archives as part of displays of the school's history in glass cabinets or for educational use.

Schoolmasters were often university graduates or clergy and so their biographies can often be uncovered in the university listings or in *Crockford's Clerical Directory* for the clergy.

For long running public schools, registers of pupils have often been published and so can be seen in major libraries. They are usually indexed by name and give a brief biography of former pupils, including the dates they attended the school and future career. Some of the old and established grammar schools also have published their listings. Some of these are online and some can be found on Ancestry.

The Derby School Register for 1570–1901 provides the following example:

'Dovaston, William D. (Jan.1871). Son of John Dovaston, Nursey, W. Felton, Shrewsbury. Played football for Upton Park, Dec. 1879. Sol. 1879, Talbot Chambers. Shrewsbury.'

Although the census returns will usually state whether a child is at school (described therein as 'scholar'), this does not tell you which school. In many cases this will be the nearest school and in villages this might well be the only school in the locality. If there are several, some can be ruled out by sex as many were for boys only or for girls only. Religious denomination is not the best guide as Anglicans might send their children to a nonconformist school if they thought the teaching was better and vice versa. For boarding schools it

Harrow Schools. *(Paul Lang's postcard)*

is even more difficult and it is not necessarily the nearest nor the one which siblings attended.

For the two ancient universities (Oxford and Cambridge) there are the multi-volume published lists of students which are arranged alphabetically. They provide biographical details such as father's name, date and place of birth of student, college/s attended, dates of matriculation and of degrees awarded, if any, and often future career and date of death. J. Foster, *Alumni Oxonienses* which covers 1500–1886 and J. and J.A. Venn, *Alumni Cantabrigienses* for 1540–1900. Both can be seen on Ancestry. There are also volumes for individual colleges too.

From the 1870s the universities of Oxford, Cambridge and Durham started to become more inclusive. In 1871 the ban on Catholics being students was lifted and female students were allowed entry with the introduction of women's colleges, although they were not always entitled to be awarded degrees until the twentieth century.

Keble College, Oxford. *(Author photograph, 2025)*

An example from Oxford university is:

Holme, James Wilson, is[sue] Samuel, of Liverpool, Lancashire, gent. Wadham COLL, Matriculated 2 Feb. 1848, aged 18. BA 1851, MA 1857.

Apart from these, there were a number of further education institutes which were established in the nineteenth century.

These mechanics' institutes were aimed at working men who wanted to improve their numeracy and literacy. They were first seen in Scotland in 1821 but their numbers soared. Some became universities and some disappeared. Existing records are held in county record offices and may list members, so could be worth a look if your working-class ancestor lived in a town which had a mechanics' institute.

If the school still exists it may be worth contacting them about any records they may have retained. The same goes for universities. Some public schools have impressive archives and these include Rugby, Winchester and Eton.

Apprenticeships

Young people, usually boys, were often made apprentices in order to learn a skilled trade in the sixteenth to eighteenth centuries, but this was generally less common in the Victorian era. The length of an apprenticeship – seven years – meant many were never completed, and the low pay and restrictions these agreements entailed on the apprentice were discouraging. However, some apprenticeship schemes did exist in the Victorian age. Pauper children were often still apprenticed when the parish paid the master to take them from the financial responsibility of the parish. Poor law unions often maintained registers of children who were apprenticed and so these can be found with poor law records at county record offices. Companies which ran apprenticeship schemes also kept registers of these youthful employees. Wood Brothers, engineers and millwrights of Yorkshire have them from 1861 to 1926, which can be seen at Calderdale Archives in Halifax. The Society of Genealogists' library has a collection of 18,000 apprenticeship indentures from 1641 to 1888. City livery companies, see below, also hold records of apprentices.

The key document is the indenture of apprenticeship when a master agrees to take on an apprentice. As a minimum this should give the name and address of each party, the date, the profession in question and the term of the apprenticeship. Each party should have kept their copies as it was a binding legal agreement into which they had both entered.

Freemen of towns and cities

Corporate towns and cities were entitled to honour those of their number with the 'freedom' of the town or city in question. This meant that certain privileges were granted to that individual. The man thus honoured would usually be a former member of the ruling body. The minutes of the body's ruling council should note this momentous event, which would probably also appear in the local press and might even be noted on a board in the town hall in their list of freemen. There were no 'freewomen' in this era.

There are also freemen of the livery companies of ancient cities. Livery companies were, and still are, organisations devoted to a particular trade, such as goldsmiths or haberdashers. In the Middle Ages they controlled entry to that particular profession only allowing freemen to do so. There were two routes to this: apprenticeship and patrimony, and records of freemen are often held at the county record office or at the livery company itself – many of those in the City of London employ a part-time archivist to administer these.

Admission papers for the freedom of the City of London can be searched on Ancestry for the years 1681–1930. There is an alphabetical list of freedoms and the admissions papers, giving brief career histories to date. So we can learn that George Evans, son of William Evans of 31 Upper Marylebone Street, Portland Place, a carver and gilder, had been apprentice to William Clowes, stationer, and was granted his freedom on 7 December 1858.

Occupations

Census returns and civil registration certificates almost always note the occupation of adults; though relatively few married women went out to work at this time. Yet the census did not usually give the name of the employer, and this is important because it is how the records of employment are organised. Of course, if your railway worker ancestor lived in Reading then the Great Western Railway is the likely employer and if the ancestor was a miner it is likely that the nearest mine employed him. The same might go for schools and hospitals, but if there are several in the town then it may be a case of checking all school/hospital records in the locality.

The occupations of some ancestors are better covered than others. Those in the armed forces are dealt with in Chapter 5. Those in work in the public sector – which was rapidly expanding in the Victorian era – or in established professions, such as the law, the church and medicine, or other occupations, are easier to trace than those who were employees in agriculture and industry or were servants, as a general rule.

Doctors can be found in *The Medical Directory*, produced annually from 1845, and *The Medical Register* from 1859. Entries are arranged alphabetically. They state which universities they attended, their qualifications, their address and even any important publications they were responsible for, and previous postings. For instance, the 1870 *Medical Directory* tells us that William Withey Gull of 26 Brooke Street, London, had registered on 1 June 1859. He had a medical degree from London University from 1846 and had been a member of the Royal College of Physicians of London from 1848. Hospital records can also list doctors on their staff, whether full time or, more frequently, part-time and honorary as an adjunct to their paid practices.

Anglican clergymen are listed in a number of annually produced publications. There are *The Clergy List* from 1841 to 1917 and *The Clergy Directory* from 1872 to 1916. From 1858 they are to be located in *Crockford's Clerical Directory*. These are arranged alphabetically. They provide details of the man's university career and then his clerical appointments at different churches or cathedrals and rank (curate, vicar, rector etc.) at each. Diocesan record offices should hold details of clergy ordained in that diocese and there should be additional information there, including educational details, baptism and character references, as well as any publications he may have written. An example is from the 1898 *Crockford's:*

'Banfather, Henry William, Blunsdon St Andrew, Highworth, Wilts – CCC Cambridge BA 1859, D. 1860 p1861 Ely, R of Blunsdon St Andr. Dio, Brist. 1887 (p. Exors of late J. Lyall esq., Gross Inc. from TRC 286l, or 217l, net 172l, pop. 93) C. of Barningham, Suffolk, 1860–62, Blunsdon, St Andr. Wilts. 1869–73. V. of Brill w. Boarstall, Oxon, 1873–87.'

Information about clergymen can also be found in the diocesan archives. These hold the induction papers when a clergyman is admitted to a benefice. Then there are the visitation returns when the bishop makes an inspection of each parish every few years; the clergyman makes a return about the religious and moral state of the parish and the churchwardens also do so, with comments about the said incumbent. Finally, there are the ecclesiastical court records where a clergyman might be tried for moral offences.

For lawyers there is the *Law List,* published from 1775. This is sub-divided, for solicitors, by the place of employment, so searching is difficult if this is not known. Barristers and other lawyers who are fewer in number, are listed as separate categories. Once the category is found then names appear alphabetically. They give qualifications and dates. For trainee lawyers there are the listings of articled clerkships from 1756 to 1874 available to search on Ancestry. The various Inns of Court have published listings of nineteenth-century barristers; some of these are available online.

Rt. Rev. Edward Bickersteth. *(Author's copy of* The Strand, *1893)*

These directories, which were published annually, often list retired members of the profession, with dates of retirement. When they cease to be listed it is usually a sign of decease. Many of these books can be found on the shelves of TNA's

Rt. Hon. Sir William Grantham. *(Author's copy of* The Strand, *1893)*

library and a selection of them can be seen on Ancestry. With an ancestor in one of these professions, it is possible to track their careers by inspecting a number of these registers until their name ceases to appear. For doctors and clergy, though not so much lawyers, Ancestry has a number of these listings to check, though very far from complete; for lawyers there is only the 1843 listing on this site.

Lesser mortals can sometimes be found in the archives. Railway workers for one, from the 1830s, can be found in the documentation of the myriad railway companies which were nationalised in the 1940s. These are mostly at TNA. The archives are organised by the name of the company that the ancestor was employed by. Some of these archives can be found on Ancestry. These cover 1833–1956 and can be searched for by name. They primarily consist of employment ledgers. These give the name of the worker, the date he was taken on by the company, his age, the position he worked in, with the weekly and annual pay, when and why he left, with any other remarks. For example, Thomas Garlick was employed by the Manchester, Sheffield and Lincolnshire Railway on 23 October 1876. He was then aged 21¾ years and was initially a goods porter, earning 19*s* per week. He became a signalman at Newton on 2 November 1879 and was dismissed on 18 March 1880 for reasons which are unstated.

Information about engineers can also be found on Ancestry. Those mechanical engineers from 1847 to 1938 are listed with names, business address, details of education and career, dates of membership with proposer and seconder. Thus, Thomas Scott Anderson, an electrical engineer and contractor of 59 Wilkinson Street, Sheffield, was aged 36 when he was proposed by James Paxman and William Ripper on 2 February 1894 as a member of the professional institute. He had previously been four years as inspector of government telegraphs in India from 1876 to 1881, then worked in Lym, America on electric lighting work from 1881 to 1888 and was subsequently employed by Compton Co. in Chelmsford.

Civil engineers can be found in the membership records of the Institute of Civil Engineers from 1820 to 1930. These provide date of membership, name of master during pupillage, number of years employed in this and other capacities and the name and address of seconders who could number ten or more existing members. Searches by name can be carried out on Ancestry.

The remit of government, whether central or local, was limited at the beginning of the nineteenth century but it rapidly expanded as the century progressed. In the 1860s and 1870s Local Boards began to be instituted. The 1888 Local Government Act led to the formation of the county councils and in 1894 Urban and Rural District Councils were formed as the second tier of local government. All these bodies took over the responsibilities of the parish vestries. Much of this was needed to combat pressing social problems resulting from rapid urbanisation and industrialisation. Government became more professional as the amateurs of the vestries were replaced by salaried officials.

There are occasionally staff books of council employees which name individuals, the department they worked in, their job title (Treasurer, Surveyor, Rate collector etc.), salary and starting date. More often, as a minimum, the names of individuals are to be found in the minute books of each department, when the employee was appointed and when they left. Promotion and transfers should also be noted. If there are any exceptional incidents in their career these are usually noted. Sometimes the minutes are indexed but not necessarily, and most are in manuscript form rather than being typed. The Ealing Staff Book for 1884–1904 for the Borough treasurer's department shows that Alfred Richardson, aged 41, earned £360 per annum, as Borough treasurer and accountant, had a month's leave and had been in post since February 1884. Benjamin Collins, one of his three assistants was aged 25, earned £110, had two weeks leave and was in post since June 1900. He would receive an extra £10 per year until a maximum of £150 had been achieved.

Senior officials and councillors will frequently appear in council minute books as attending various committee meetings and may be noted as having spoken at meetings. These were often reported in local newspapers in great detail as well as in the manuscript minutes. So in the minutes of the works committee, implementing infrastructure and discussing whether builders' plans should be authorised, the borough or county surveyor should be present as well as the councillors who made up the committee.

Although the Metropolitan Police was established in 1829 for London, county police forces were not compulsory until 1856. There are many archives covering policemen and their careers, which records may be held at the appropriate county record office, and though there are extensive closure periods (100 years for Devon and Cornwall), for personnel in the Victorian era there is no such problem. For the Metropolitan Police there is an alphabetical list of joiners from 1830 to 1857 and then from 1878 to 1933. These give dates of joining and leaving, rank, division and warrant number. Certificates of service from 1889 to 1909 provide information about their careers. Registers of men leaving from 1889 to 1947 can be searched for by name online at the Discovery site. Those who died in service from 1829 to 1889 can be found at MEPO4/2 which is indexed and gives cause of death. Pension records cover 1852–1923 and these give a brief biography of the pensioner, with place and date of birth, date of commencement of service and any promotions and changes of division, as well as a physical description of the man on leaving the service (his hair was usually greying). Next of kin are given.

Another branch of public service for which records survive is the Post Office. As with the police there are appointment records and pension records. Some of these have been digitised and can be searched for on Ancestry as they are held centrally. Appointment books from 1737 to 1969 and

Policeman. *(Paul Lang's postcard)*

pension and gratuity records for 1861–70 can be searched by name on Ancestry. Frank Brailsford was appointed as a junior letter sorter in Manchester on February 1880 for example. Meanwhile, Thomas Henry Bignell, having been appointed on 30 September 1853 left on 12 February 1881, as a letter carrier. His finishing salary was £86 0*d*, including £7 16*s* 5*d* allowance for his good conduct stripes.

The careers of senior civil servants, are, as with those for army and naval officers, easier to find because they are listed in the annually produced *British Imperial Calendar* from 1809 to 1972 and the *Royal Kalendar* from 1767 to 1890. Incomplete runs of these can be found in TNA's library. The *Foreign Office List* covers the period 1852–1965, and the *Colonial Office List* covers 1862–1966 and provides listings per year of senior civil servants, whose career history can be traced through these volumes. Their histories, as with those of army and navy officers, can also be traced in *The London Gazette* of official appointments, and which can be searched online for free.

Despite the railway mania of the 1840s, the eighteenth- and early nineteenth-century network of canals were still well used for industrial transport throughout the country. Wage and salary books for canal employees are sometimes held at TNA but mostly at the county record offices where the company was based. Those for the Staffordshire and Worcestershire Canal Navigation Company after 1875 are at Gloucestershire Archives.

County and local directories, discussed further in Chapter 8, often list the names of councillors, magistrates, MPs and senior council officials in their introductory surveys. As these surveys were often produced annually they can be used to find starting and leaving dates, and addresses.

The archives of some businesses survive, either kept by the business if it still exists or having been deposited at the appropriate record office where that business was located. If a businessman went bankrupt they can be traced in *The London Gazette* as bankruptcy notices are listed there.

It is often difficult to find out more about an ancestor's working life beyond the bare references on the census, civil registration certificates and parish registers. One instance is the case of domestic servants, which was the most common occupation for women in Victorian Britain. In 1851 there were almost a million servants in Britain; 1.23 million in 1881 and 1.33 million in 1901. Some were male but because they had to be paid more and because there was a male servant tax in England until 1937, the majority were women.

The bad news is that most servants were employed in middle-class households which had only one or two servants. However, the minority who were employed in large establishments like grand town houses, as in the TV series *Upstairs Downstairs*, or country houses à la *Downton Abbey* (though both dramas are set in the post Victorian era) are better recorded. Estate records, found in county record offices, or sometimes still at the house itself if still in the same family, can include relevant papers.

The records in question are wages, livery and pension books. Wages were once paid annually but by the end of our period would be more likely to be paid quarterly. Livery refers to the uniforms servants were obliged to wear when at work and the employer had to provide these and their replacements. These books name the servant, their role and their wage/pension (an annuity might be paid or a weekly wage and this might be transferred to the widow/er) if retired. It is possible to trace how a servant advanced in their career by job title and wage paid. So if you know where they worked, via census returns, then it should be possible to seek out where any record relating to their employers will be kept. The West Sussex Record Office, for example, has servants registers for the Goodwood Estate from 1869 to 1927.

There are also receipts for pay and these were usually when the employer, through his land agent, paid the wages and the servant signed a slip confirming receipt. Sir T.F. Fremantle's wage receipts for his staff from 1863 to 1865 can be found in the Centre for Buckinghamshire Studies. However, these are typically for only short runs of years.

Another source for all servants are the wills of their employers. These often record setting aside sums for favoured or longstanding servants and so may be a clue to length of service and / or how well thought of that particular servant was.

Trade Unions

From being banned in the late eighteenth century, unions were given legal recognition in 1825 but development was slow and in 1833 a plan for the Grand National Trade Union was a failure. The first large-scale union was the Amalgamated Society of Engineers in 1851. Initially, unions were more concerned about the social benefits to their members than with trade disputes. The Trade Union Congress was formed in 1868 and in 1875 peaceful picketing was legalised. There were important disputes in later years such as the London Dock strike in 1889. Even so, membership was relatively low and by 1895 only about 1.5 million of the workforce were union members.

Having said that, some industries saw significant increases in union membership. By 1900 there were just over 62,000 railwaymen who were union members, up from under 9,000 in 1880, and many other skilled professions became increasingly unionised. Among these were engineers, carpenters, joiners, boilermakers, ironmakers, steam engine makers, iron founders and bricklayers. The postal workers' union founded in 1891 had over 20,000 members in 1900.

The majority of union members were listed in union admission books and received membership cards. The former should include details such as the new member's name, age, date of admission, number of years in the trade, marital status and nominated next of kin to receive funeral benefits. Dates of existing records vary by union. Those for the Amalgamated Society of Carpenters and Joiners only date from 1895, and those of the Amalgamated Society of Railway Servants from 1897 (though including existing members from earlier years), but those of the Amalgamated Society of House Decorators and Painters begin in 1873.

Warwick University's Modern Records Society hold some of the archives of trades unions, but they can also be found at county record offices.

Some union members were more active and acted as officials; more can be learnt about them as they feature in the minute books of union branch committee meetings. Those attending the meetings will be recorded, the post each man held should be there, as might the contributions they made at meetings. Branch returns and annual reports were compiled by the branches to the union executive and these should also provide information about union officials.

The People's History Museum in Manchester is another important source for trade union archives. They include archives for the boilermakers' union and those for the clothing industries. The TUC Library collection holds searchable delegate lists for each TUC congress since 1868 and these can be searched on their website, The Union Makes Us Strong. There are also strike pay lists for the famous Bryant and May strike of 1888 in East London. The National Library of Scotland holds some union records for Scotland.

Freemasonry

The United Grand Lodge of English Freemasons membership registers cover 1751–1921 and can be viewed on Ancestry. They provide names, age and year of birth, occupations, addresses and date of membership. Anthony Smith, for example, was born in 1843, and was initiated as a lodge member at the age of 32, on 14 July 1875. He was a contractor and was a member of the Arboretum Lodge in Derby.

Listings of freemasons can be found among county quarter session records in the county record offices. Lodges were obliged to send membership lists to the magistrates for fear that such a society might be seditious and those for Warwickshire from 1799 to 1850 can be searched on Ancestry.

The lodge provided a list of names, with title and profession and place of abode for each year.

There is also the Museum of Freemasonry at the Freemasons' Hall at 60 Great Queen Street, London, which includes year books listing freemasons, though occupations are not given. They are open for researchers. Apart from archives relating to masons, there are also some for several friendly societies as well there.

Chapter 4

RELIGIOUS AFFILIATION

Britain's religious diversity was more open in the Victorian era than in previous centuries. The former legal restrictions on Catholic and nonconformist worship were now over. It should also be noted that the Anglican Church's role in local government was vastly decreased following the 1834 New Poor Law which removed the parish vestry's responsibility for the poor – though not the payments ratepayers had to make. The established church, though, was still an important social and religious institution. Parish registers apart, church archives are still a significant source for family historians.

Parish registers and civil registration certificates should tell you where these crucial life events took place and so this should give the Christian denomination of your ancestor. As a generalisation, many Irish ancestors would have been Catholic and many Welsh, nonconformist. However, this was not always so, and it is not axiomatic that their children would be brought up in the same faith as their parents. Herbert Mahon was born in 1888 in Liverpool and his father had been born in Dublin (it is not known whether he was Catholic or Protestant). The young Mahon was baptised at St Peter's Anglican church and attended a Church of England school.

Church of England

However, whether your ancestors liked it or not they were still to an extent (far lesser than in previous centuries) involved in the Church of England; all wills up to 1858 were dealt with in church courts for example, and the Anglican Vestry still levied rates on the population for much of this period. In terms of religion the country was divided, as it was from the Middle Ages, into two archdioceses: Canterbury (covering the south of England and the Midlands) and York (covering the north of England). These are then sub-divided into dioceses, each headed by a bishop based at a cathedral. As population expanded in the nineteenth century some of the ancient dioceses had new dioceses carved out from them. Manchester became a diocese in 1847 and Wakefield in 1888.

Each diocese was divided into archdeaconries and then parishes, each with a parish church and a minister, usually a rector or vicar. The two main record-creating bodies were the diocese and the parish and their archives have been mostly kept at county record offices since at least the 1970s. Very few churches have any records other than those in current or very recent use, though some do have copies of older records, such as those at Kidwelly church in Carmarthenshire.

The population of Victorian England vastly increased, especially in the towns and cities. This led to an increase in the number of churches in places where there had been just one. Having said this, attendance at Anglican churches was a minority pastime; in 1851, some 5,292,551 people did so regularly – about 20 per cent of the population.

Vestry minute books are one of the most important records created by the churches. These are records of the formal meetings, often monthly, of the body, who administered the church's activities. They list those who attended these meetings and the decisions they took. After 1834 these focused on the upkeep of the church fabric and on the

Thomas a Becket's chapel, Wymondham. *(Paul Lang's postcard)*

distribution of funds from charities to recipients. The major church officials were much as they had always been for most of this period, namely: two churchwardens, two overseers and a surveyor of the highways. These were annual and unpaid appointments. Parish constables became fewer and fewer with the introduction of professional police forces.

The New Poor Law had taken away some of the responsibility for the poor from the parish. But overseers were still appointed until 1925. They were obliged to assess the rateable value of parochial properties and to set and collect rates. Some parishes continued to give what was termed 'outdoor relief'. Norwood Overseers' accounts and payments list a number of individuals who were relieved in the 1870s. They are listed for each week by surname, and the same surnames appear on a number of occasions. Sometimes more than one family was being relieved, so there is Bryant, Mrs Bryant and Bryant Boy. The amount of money given was also noted and this often varied. In the case of the Bryants the amounts were 15 shillings, 2 shillings and 9 shillings respectively. It would also seem that some of these people worked for their money. For example, Willis received 12*s* 6*d* and a further 7*s* for 'thatching'. Nicholls Boy was given 9 shillings for 'harvest work'.

Vestry members and officials are often mentioned in these minutes when topics for action and discussion take place. A resolution taken in the Hanwell vestry in 1879 was as follows:

> It was moved by Mr Walter Abbott; seconded by Mr T. Paul and carried unanimously,
>
> 1. that the meeting has heard with feelings of the greatest indignation the letter addressed by Mr William White to the Reverend James Greaves which it regards as an act of tyranny and supererogation, and is moreover, of the opinion that the spiritual needs of the members of the Church of England in this parish, particularly those of the poor – will be most efficiently met by a continuation of his ministry.
>
>   It was moved by Dr Burton; seconded by Mr Bramsgrove and carried unanimously
>
> 2. That this meeting most cordially supports, and in the most emphatic manner, the memorial signed by a very large majority, of the adult inhabitants of this parish, but is of opinion that such an expression of confidence in the Reverend James Greaves renders an enquiry unnecessary by the Bishop of the Diocese.
>
>   It was moved by Mr J. Morris seconded by Mr E. West and carried unanimously
>
> 3. That this meeting is of opinion that possible effort should be made to defeat the attempt to coerce the Rector in his selection or nomination of an

> incumbent, or curate in charge, to the proposed new church of St Mark and that this object can only be fully obtained by the resignation of Rudolph Spearman, Esq., E.W. Mansell Esq., and William White Esq., of their respective offices of parish clerk, churchwarden and sidesman and architect for the new church and also their connection with the church building committee.

There were still other secular matters that the church dealt with. In some cases, their powers increased. The Metropolis Local Management Act of 1855 gave parishes in the vicinity of London much more to do if they chose to (Hampstead vestry formed a dozen committees after this date and they continued to exist until taken over by the metropolitan borough of Hampstead in 1900). Although no longer administering the poor law after 1834, parishes still had to make rating assessments and collect money from the ratepayers to remit to the poor law union. Highways were still a parish responsibility until the late nineteenth century, and there were new responsibilities such as matters relating to sanitary business: burials, sewers and more generally, as well as lighting. These meant that additional committees needed to be formed to deal with these challenges.

Highway rate books continued to be kept until the end of the era, when secular bodies took over the maintenance of the roads, so no more highway rates from the vestry. From 1868 the compulsory church rate was abolished, given the increasing diversity in Christian worship as nonconformists and Catholics objected. Rate books are important because they list the householders in a parish and their financial liabilities; these will be discussed in more detail later.

Pew rents also led to the creation of archives by the parish. This was a system where churchgoers paid to guarantee them having a particular pew to sit in during the church service. Middle- and lower-middle-class people often paid for this and it was an important source of revenue in many churches. By the later nineteenth century this practice was in decline. The records will list payees, dates begun and finished and amounts and location. If there is a plan then you might even be able to find the pew that your ancestor used – unless the church has replaced its pews with chairs.

Churches ran Sunday Schools to teach children about the Bible and their faith in a mix of lessons and other activities suitable to their year group; it was not uncommon for children to be divided by age as per orthodox schools. These often took place on Sunday afternoons. Registers were kept of those attending and the best attenders were often awarded with a prize at the year's end. A cynic might argue that these were used by parents who wanted some peace from their children on a Sunday afternoon. Registers list children attending and so this is a useful source for ancestors' childhoods.

Confirmation registers often exist. These are chronological lists of people who, having been baptised, wanted to take the next step in their journey of Christian faith by being confirmed as young people or as adults. This involves additional instruction and learning. It leads to a ceremony with the bishop at a church service to mark this important step. The confirmation register will thus show that an ancestor was still attending this particular church and that on a certain date he or she was confirmed, as well as the fact that they took their faith seriously and had taken a conscious decision to do so, as opposed to baptism where that decision is taken by parents and to an extent might be for tradition or social reasons. These registers are less common than parish registers and some may include decades' worth of entries.

Parish magazines began to be composed at the end of the Victorian period and these can be useful sources of information. They often list the principal people involved in the work of the parish, as well as the clergy. Parishes often organised a great deal of social and sporting activities. The parish magazines for St Mary's church, Ealing, in 1890, list the two clergymen and the two churchwardens, with addresses; the nine sidesmen (though surnames only of these helpers and no addresses); the organist; parish clerk and collector of charities. Then there is a list of the baptisms, marriages and burials for the preceding month with names, dates and in the case of baptisms, addresses and for burials, age. Then there is information about church activities and the individuals who took a lead in them. These included a children's prizegiving event and those awarding prizes were named. At a musical event, those who sang or gave recitals were named. As there had recently been an appeal for building a new Sunday School, the names of donors with amounts given was published.

Southall parish magazines for the 1880s also list the schoolchildren who won school attendance awards, listing them by school. As these school registers are not known to survive this allows a researcher to know which school their ancestor attended, at least if their ancestors were assiduous school attenders.

There are many miscellaneous archives within parish archives. Norwood had an 1863 parish valuation, providing a snapshot of the properties' inhabitants at that time.

Archives are held at the county or borough archives in their role as appointed diocesan record office. Most cathedrals have their own archives, like as Exeter Cathedral, and there is Lambeth Palace Library which covers the archdiocese of Canterbury, and the Borthwick Centre for Archives, part of York University, covers that for York. The latter also holds many parish archives, not just those for York but for many other Yorkshire parishes. Very few parish archives are available online, with the exception of the registers of baptisms, marriages and deaths.

It is always worth checking the parish archive for the parish in which your ancestor lived, regardless of whether or not they were Anglican. Because until 1894, in addition to being an ecclesiastical unit, the parish was also the lowest tier of local government. Nonconformists, Catholics and Jews were not obliged to attend the Anglican church for worship but they were obliged to pay the rates that the church vestry set and so some would attend vestry meetings to have their say in expenditure.

Nonconformist churches

Nonconformity has existed from the time of the Reformation, and more so since the seventeenth century. From 1689 these Protestant Dissenters were still under legal restrictions for worship (though less so than previously) and thereafter were barred from many professions in the state which required an oath of allegiance to the monarch as Head of State. By the Victorian era most of these had been lifted. Non-Anglican Protestant denominations were Methodists (Primitive, Wesleyan and Unitarian), founded in the eighteenth century, as well as the earlier forms of Dissent – the Baptists, Congregationalists, Presbyterians and Quakers, to name the most prominent. There were also some smaller sects such as the Plymouth Brethren and Moravians.

In 1851 some 4,536,265 people regularly attended chapel, with chapel-going being particularly strong in Wales, where 80 per cent of those who regularly attended a place of worship went to chapel. These were Protestants who did not acknowledge the monarch as the head of their church (nor the Pope, of course). Nor did they have bishops or the wealth that the established Anglican Church had accumulated over the centuries.

Many of the archives already referred to as being created by the Anglican Church are applicable here, such as with pew rent registers, Sunday School and confirmation registers.

Regarding property, most of these churches had trustees who managed the property belonging to the church or chapel, similar perhaps to the Anglican churchwardens, and were usually senior and older members of the male congregation. The minute books will list attenders and their decisions, and often mention who was the lead and seconder.

By the early Victorian era Methodism had overtaken the early forms of nonconformist worship. Methodist chapels were organised into circuits. The former held quarterly meetings of the ministers which were recorded in minute books. Chapel administration was entrusted to trustees. Congregationalists were formed into the Congregational Union of England and Wales in 1831. Many Baptist churches were part of the Baptist New Connexion as well as the mainstream General Assembly of Baptists after 1770 before they and others came together as the Baptist Union of Great Britain and Ireland. In Scotland there was the Scottish Episcopalian Church, with archives at the National Records of Scotland.

Sometimes there are lists of deeds and trustees which give, year by year, the names of the latter, their addresses and occupations. That for the Ealing and Acton circuit covers 1865–1920. So for 1887 we find that the trustees included Henry John Atkinson esquire, of Gunnersbury, Acton. Henry Collier was next and he was of Bollo Bridge, a laundryman. Others included shopkeepers. All were men.

As with Anglican churches, they kept baptism, marriage and burial registers. Sometimes there were lists of church members with addresses and these were often updated if members left the district or died or new members joined. Barnet Archives has a church roll from 1833 to 1917 for the Edgware Congregational church, for example, and this denomination seems to have been particularly enthusiastic about keeping records. Circuits cross local authority boundaries so you might have to check at more than one record office for these.

The Society of Friends' Library has the following sources. There are the Quaker Digests, which are alphabetical listings of the marriages and deaths of Quakers, the Annual Monitor from 1613 to 1920, which are annual listings of deceased Quakers and give information about their lives and deaths (an index is available), testimonies of deceased preachers (1837–1867), and Books of Sufferings, 1659–1857. Locally are the proceedings of regularly held meetings, which are accounts of the work undertaken that year and obituaries of local prominent Quakers.

Their records, as with those of the Anglican Church, tend to be held in county and borough archives, though some baptism, marriage and burial registers are held at TNA. That being said, the Baptists do not believe in baptising infants, only adults, and so baptism registers are rather different than they are for other Christian denominations. Many nonconformist archives are also to be found at Dr Williams' Library at 14 Gordon Square, London.

Catholic churches

Catholic worship had become legal at the end of the eighteenth century with additional steps taken to greater emancipation in 1829, but it was very much a minority denomination in the Victorian era (except for Ireland, which was predominantly Catholic). In 1850 the Catholic hierarchy was re-established in Britain with Cardinal Newman at Westminster and twelve dioceses throughout the country. From 1850 to 1865 the number of priests trebled and monasteries were founded. In 1851 some 383,630 people (about 2 per cent of the population) regularly attended Catholic churches in mainland Britain and many who did so were Irish or had Irish roots in places like Liverpool and London.

By the Victorian period the state took less interest in Catholics, but there are some registers of Catholics attesting their loyalty to the state as late as 1857. These can be found at TNA, reference E169/83, giving names and addresses.

Records of Catholic churches are either held at the church or at the record office which covers that district. Relatively few are held at the Westminster Diocese Archives.

There are also the publications of the *Catholic Record Society*, many of them freely available online. For example, the volume for 2001 gives biographies of major Catholic benefactors from 1667 to 2000. The volume of the 'Letters of Dr John Lingard to Mrs Thomas Lomax' cover 1835–50 and were published in 2000.

Prominent Catholics can be found in the five volume *A Literary and Biographical Dictionary of the English Catholics from the breach with Rome to the Present time*, by Joseph Gillow in 1885–1902. It is arranged alphabetically and most of the entries are to men and many are to priests. One entry is as follows:

> Morton, Thomas Naylor, palaeographer, was born March 3, 1816, at Sibsey, Lincolnshire, where his father, Thomas Morton, owned an estate, and was known as a keen sportsman, as a great gardener and agriculturist, and as a voluminous poet; he was, besides, the author of a 'Life of St Francis of Assisi' and of a work on the Holy Trinity.
>
> Morton was educated at Durham University, took orders, and was a curate for some years at Cirencester, West Houghton (Lancashire), Harlow (Essex), and Devizes. He was received into the Church by Cardinal Newman in 1853.
>
> On July 17, 1858, he married Augusta, eldest daughter of Thomas Champion, of Hatfield, Herts, who survived him, and by whom he left three sons and two daughters, the latter being respectively superioress at the Convent of Mercy, Handsworth, Birmingham, and prioress of the Good Shepherd Convent, Dalbeith, Glasgow.

Uniquely, there is the 1893 Westminster diocesan census for London Catholics. Apart from all the usual information that would be expected from a census, it also gives the priests' comments on the moral character of each Catholic, which gives an additional insight into the character of the ancestor in question. This can be viewed on FindMyPast.

Finally, we should not forget the minority of non-Christian believers. These were at this time primarily the small Jewish communities, mostly in places such as London, Manchester and Leeds. They were the last of the religious minorities to gain full civil rights. Some were very socially prominent, like the Rothschilds and Disraelis. Synagogue archives are usually held at the appropriate county or borough record office. Sometimes additional permission is needed to view these. Apart from registers of marriages and burials there are also registers of circumcisions (no baptism registers, of course). Many are held at the university of Southampton but are privately owned. (Chapter 9 deals with the substantial Jewish immigration in the mid- to late nineteenth century.)

Chapter 5

WAR AND PEACE

Although there was no general European war between 1815 and 1914 there were numerous smaller conflicts, mostly with non-European powers, in which the British army and Royal Navy were engaged. There were wars in Asia (the Chinese wars, the Afghan wars of 1839–1840, 1878 and 1880 and the India Mutiny of 1857–1858), Africa (the Ashanti campaign, the Zulu War of 1879 and the Boer wars of 1880 and 1899–1902) and New Zealand, as the British Empire expanded. The only major European power which Britain fought was Russia, in the Crimean war of 1854–1855. It meant that there was no form of conscription and so all recruitment into the armed forces was voluntary. There were three main branches of the armed forces: the regular army, the Royal Navy, and the volunteer forces – some of whom also served abroad.

Army

The army was administered by the War Office and was divided into infantry, cavalry and artillery. The infantry and cavalry were divided into regiments, the artillery into Field and Horse Artillery, and there were also the Household or Guards regiments based in London and Windsor. Until 1858 there was also the army of the East India Company in India; replaced by the (British) Indian Army until 1947.

The principal repository for army archives is The National Archives. It is easier to locate officers than it is for the rank and file. The *Army Lists*, published annually from 1754 and then quarterly from 1879, are an essential first port of call because they give basic details of an officer's career. They are arranged by regiment and indexed by name. They provide dates of commission and promotions. After 1879 they are listed by seniority, and after 1881 they give a man's war service. Army lists can be found on the shelves of TNA's library.

The 1839 *Army List*, for example, tells us that Sir D. Cunninghame Bt., late of the 82nd Foot (to pick a random name off the list) was appointed to a colonelcy on 26 January 1797. In itself this is not much, but you could then go back to the list for 1796 and check his rank then and when he was appointed to it and work your way back.

A couple of quick ways to find army artillery and engineer officers are: first, the *List of officers of the Royal Regiment of Artillery* from 1716 to 1899 by J. Kane, and second, a like volume by T.W.J. Connolly, *List of the Officers of the Corps of Royal Engineers, 1660–1899*.

Army officers can also be searched for name at Discovery for the years 1764–1913. These are organised by regiment and give name, age, dates of first commission in the army and of current appointment, country of origin, the name of the predecessor officer and remarks, which is usually a comment on when and by what means their service ended. An example could be from majors of the 2nd battalion of the 8th Regiment of Foot, J.D.C. Hamilton, whose first army commission was dated 3 September 1842, he was born in Scotland, current appointment on 23 January 1863, when aged 37 years 8 months, and who retired on half pay on 1 September 1868. (Please note: this searching method brings up the document for the regiment in which there is an index at the beginning to names, rather than the man's details immediately.)

Colonel Frederick Roberts. *(Author's copy of* The Strand, *1893)*

Up to 1870 most promotions were purchased. WO31 lists the commander in chief's memorandum of appointments, promotions and resignations from 1793. The Secretary at War's correspondence on the same is in WO4/513-520 from 1704 to 1858. *The London Gazette* also gives dates of appointments to commissions.

Men leaving the service usually went on half pay (pensions did not exist until 1871) and so could theoretically be called up for future service. Ledgers of these men are in record series PMG4, (1737–1921) and from 1841 the ledgers are arranged alphabetically by name so searching is far easier. Bounties paid to officers' widows from 1815 to 1856 are to be found in WO25/3069-3072 and are indexed.

Births, marriage and burial certificates for officers' children from 1755 to 1908 can be searched for on Ancestry.

Courts martial for commissioned officers were held by general or field courts martial. These are in series WO71/121-343 for 1668–1879.

Many men becoming infantry and cavalry officers had been to the Royal Military Academy at Sandhurst as cadets. There is a database of these men on the Sandhurst Academy website covering the years 1783–1964 which can be searched for a fee.

Rank and File

For the more numerous men in the ranks it is helpful to know the name of the regiment in which he served because that is how the records are organised. Pay and muster rolls are the crucial documents and there are a number of these.

For the majority of soldiers from 1732 to 1878, WO12 is the series to be searched. However, for artillery the series are WO10, 54, 69, for engineers it is WO11 and 54, for the Crimean War, WO14. For the years 1878–1898 it is WO16 for all soldiers. By this time regiments were known by names; they had been known as numbers hitherto, usually now by the name of a county or district, such as the South Wales Borderers.

Then there are description books, giving men's name, place of birth, previous trade, age and service, and are at reference WO25/266-688. They cover 1756–1900 but are incomplete for the later nineteenth century. These can be searched by name via TNA website. Descriptions of sappers from 1768 to 1908 are at WO67, for men of the Royal Artillery from 1749 to 1863 and 1873–6 in WO54/260-309 and WO69/74-80, and for the Royal Horse Artillery from 1803 to 1863.

British soldiers at Dehli Gate, India. *(Paul Lang's postcard)*

There are also records of courts martial. These are of two types, the District Courts martial (WO86) from 1829 to 1979 and the General Courts martial (WO92) from 1806 to 1930. These can be searched for online on Ancestry but the actual record cannot be seen there. Information gives basic details, so from WO86/456 we can learn that Private John Murray of the second battalion of the Leicester Regiment was tried on 28 August 1896 for having struck a soldier. The trial was at Malta and the sentence was eighty-four days with twenty-eight days being remitted. On the same day and at the same place, Gunner R. Collingham of the Royal Artillery was tried for striking a superior (a bombardier) and he was given the higher sentence of one year and six months; remitted twenty-eight days. It is not recorded who was assaulted and the circumstances surrounding the incident. There are also the records of the Judge Advocate General at WO91 for 1806–1904 and WO93/1a provides an index to the WO91 series. Registers for 1760–1960 and 1806–1960 can be found in respectively WO90 and WO92. For India the registers are at WO88 from 1878 to 1948 and for London from 1865 to 1875 at WO87.

British Military and Naval courts martial registers from 1806 to 1930 can be searched online on Ancestry. They give the name of the man, his unit, and the date and place of the court martial; thus, for example, William Johnson of the Rifle Brigade, tried at Winchester on 4 April 1862.

Some men deserted and they can be initially found on UK military deserters on Ancestry and searched by name to provide basic details of name, place and year of birth, unit and date and place of court martial. An example could be John Matthews, born in Dublin in about 1830 and a member of the Royal Lancaster Regiment. He was tried for desertion on 3 November 1881 at Liverpool. However, the full record can only be seen online at Forces Records for a fee.

For meritorious soldiers there were medals for gallantry and also campaign medals for all those who served. Medals for the years 1793–1949 can be searched on Ancestry by name, giving name of recipient, name of medal, regiment and result. William Bignell of the 57th Regiment was in South Africa between 1877 and 1879, and was awarded the South African Campaign medal. He went into the reserves after his period of military service.

Pension records are also important. The Chelsea Hospital was founded in the 1670s and wounded and disabled soldiers could claim pensions as either 'in pensioners' or as 'out pensioners'. Admission registers from 1702 to 1980 give details of these men. They can be searched for by name on Ancestry. An example is Thomas Jones, born in Carlisle in about 1830 and admitted pensioner on 11 August 1857. He had served for two and a half years in the Royal Canadian Rifles.

Breach in the Cashmere Gate during the Indian Mutiny. *(Paul Lang's postcard)*

National Commemoration Medal of the Transvaal Campaign. *(Paul Lang's postcard)*

There are very few records of soldiers who became prisoners of war. Some men who were captured in the Crimean and second Anglo-Boer wars had their names published in *The London Gazette*, which can be searched online, though this is restricted to officers. There is a listing of casualties in the latter war and this includes all ranks, and includes men taken prisoner as well as being killed or wounded. This can be searched for by name on Ancestry. It brings up name, rank, regiment, fate, and date of occurrence. One example is J. Holmes, prisoner of war, a corporal in the 68th battery of the Royal Field Artillery, released at Dewetsdorp on 23 November 1900.

Memorial inscriptions in churches and cathedrals sometimes commemorate the career and life of officers. Men from the ranks are rarely commemorated thus, though some are: the Maiwand Lion memorial in Reading, for example, commemorates the officers and men killed at Maiwand in 1880, and also in memorials to the 2nd Boer war.

There are also museums and other specialist repositories catering for army history such as the National Army Museum, the Guards Museum in London and regimental museums. These generally do not hold archives of individual soldiers, but it is certainly worth contacting the regimental museum for the corps in which an ancestor is known to have served, if only to establish the context in which he existed.

The East India Company maintained its own armed forces, officered by Britons and manned by Indians up to 1858. The East India year books, produced annually from 1823 to 1868 can be viewed in the library of TNA. These year books list, by district, both army officers and civilian officials, with names, posts held and from when. In 1858–1947 the Crown administered the Empire in India and the armed forces there were known as the Indian Army. From 1868 these volumes were known as the India Lists and provided the same function. As with the regular army regiments, the Indian Army could serve outside India as well as locally, and fought alongside units of the regular army in campaigns such as the battle of Maiwand in 1880. East India Company service and pension records can be accessed on FindMyPast and at the main archive at the British Library in the Asia, Pacific and African collection. Indian Army Lists can be seen at the latter from 1889 to 1947. The Lists include a man's date of birth, date of joining the regiment, current rank and date of gaining his commission.

For the Boer war of 1899 to 1902 there is a database of those who served on FindMyPast, which will give rank, battalion, wounds, medals and location of service. So for Dr Arthur Conan Doyle, we learn that he was employed as a surgeon at Langman's Field Hospital.

Royal Navy

Although there were no major set-piece naval battles in this period, unlike those of Trafalgar in 1805 or Jutland in 1916, the Royal Navy was busy in the Victorian era. They were involved in escorting transport ships of troops to the various wars like those in the Crimea, or supported land actions, such as at Omdurman in 1898. They were also involved in independent actions such as the Africa squadron, which worked to suppress slavery off Africa. The Royal Navy was made up of the officers and ratings who comprised the ships' companies.

Officers are easier to trace than men because they are, as with army officers, named in published listings, the *Navy List*, which dates from 1814, which can be seen on the shelves of TNA's library. They are arranged by ship, listing officers and the date that they obtained their present rank. There are also listings of other officer ranks such as surgeons, retired officers and Royal Marine officers. For example the *Navy List* for December 1882 for HMS *Pembroke* lists the 14 officers from captain to boatswain and four additional officers for the ship which was then at Chatham dockyard.

The *Biographia Navalis* was published in 1849 and listed in alphabetical order officers then serving and retired officers, with a career history of each man. It can be seen on Ancestry. One entry is as follows:

> BATE (LIEUTENANT, 1841, F-P, 16, H-P, 0)
> WILLIAM THORNTON BATE entered the Navy 2 Sept. 1831, passed his examination on 1 May 1839; served as Mate on board the BLENHEIM 72, Capt. Thos. Herbert, and Wellesley 72, bearing the broad pedant of Sir Gordon Bremer; and for his service during the operation of May 1841, against Canton, where he was wounded, was awarded a commission, dated on 8 of the following Oct. As additional lieutenant of the Bentinck 10, Capt. Rich. Collinson, he was subsequently employed on shore at the landing the troops, he accompanied them in their advance, and by his spirited exertions succeeded in making prisoner a Chinese officer holding the rank of colonel. He next searched with Capt Collinson on board the PLOVER surveying vessel, and since 8 July 1843 has been in command, also in the East Indies, of the YOUNG HEBE tender.

For naval ratings in the early Victorian period and from 1667 to 1878 there are two main sources of information. The first are the ships' musters, which are crew lists of who sailed on a certain ship on a certain voyage. The problem is, you need to know the name of the ship that he sailed on, and to bear in mind that he may have served on other ships, as the muster will only give his name and rank. Age and description were often included from the 1830s. Ships' muster rolls can be searched on Discovery.

However, sailors, who were always paid in arrears, were encouraged to make wills and many of them did, in contrast to the bulk of the country's working-class population. These wills can be searched by name of the sailor on TNA's website. When found they give not only the names of the beneficiaries of the will but also, and crucially, the name of the ship the man served on. This then leads the researcher on to the appropriate ships' muster rolls. These wills were proved in the Prerogative Court of Canterbury. There is also the naval wills register of 1786–1861, in ADM48/1-105, which gives the name, address and occupation of the will's executor, which is usually their next of kin. One such was John Brown, a seaman and quartermaster, of the 72-gun ship *Benbow*. His money went to one Charlotte Brown, a spinster of 3, Castle Row on the Green, Gosport, Hampshire. This was probably his sister. ADM154 covers men killed, or who died in service, in 1858–1879

From 1853 there is a centralised list of naval ratings. These are the Continuous Service Engagement Books of ADM139 and from 1873 the registers of seamen's services in ADM188. These records can be searched on TNA's website by name. They can show year and place of birth, name of ship(s) served on with dates of joining and discharge, period of service, service number. Those in ADM139 should note whether a man had served in the Merchant Navy.

After 1892 there may be additional details of each man. These include prior occupation, good conduct medals (if any), comments about the man's character and ability, physical appearance, wounds and death (if applicable). Promotion, if any, to warrant officer, should also be noted.

An example is Matthew Grier Sinclair. He was born on 28 July 1864 in South Shields, Durham. He joined at New Brighton on 29 August 1899 and his first ship was the *Colossus*; his last the *Western*. He was a boatsman, 5 feet 8 inches high, dark brown hair, blue eyes and a fair complexion. He had a tattoo on his left arm, a coat of arms on his right arm and a mark in his left thumb. He left the service in 1909 because of defective vision.

After 1894 each man is assigned a number and this will correspond to his branch of service within the Royal Navy. These include seamen and communications ratings, engine room artificers, stokers, artisans, sick berth staff, stewards, cooks and servants.

Certificates of service, ADM29, are another source for men between about 1804 and 1894. These can be found on Ancestry in full and in part on TNA's site and are proofs of a man's service, giving dates of his service and on which ship(s). Allotment registers for the period 1830–52 at ADM27 can be searched for by name on the TNA's site and these provide information about the ship served aboard, next of kin, home address and children. Medal rolls from 1793 to 1972 can be searched on Ancestry. Reginald A. Laycock of HMS *Terrible,* was, after the Boer War, awarded the Queen's and the King's South African Medals.

Pension records are another major source. From 1789 to 1894 these can be searched for by name on TNA's site. They include information from admissions into Greenwich Maritime Hospital and applications for men's children in to the Greenwich Hospital School.

The Royal Navy Reserve was formed in 1859 of experienced officers and men from the Merchant Navy to act as a reserve in case of war, and by 1890 they numbered 20,000. To research officers from 1862 to 1964, ADM240, which can be searched by name on TNA's site, can bring up the following details. Name, date and place of birth, rank, date of seniority and promotions, training undertaken, ships served on, with dates of joining and discharge, period of time served and home address. ADM340 is another source, as are the *Navy Lists*. Unfortunately, only a small sample of naval ratings' records survive before 1908. These can be searched for in BT164 and can be searched for on the TNA site Discovery.

There are also the Royal Marines, those soldiers who sailed on ships, founded in 1664 and made permanent in 1755. They were then based in Chatham, Plymouth and Portsmouth. In 1855 the Royal Marine Light Infantry force was created in addition to these. Officers can be found in the *Navy Lists* and appointments in *The London Gazette*. Service records from 1793 to 1925 can be downloaded from the TNA site, covering ADM196 and in the seniority list covering 1760–1886 from ADM192/1-44.

FindMyPast has marriage registers for the Portsmouth and Chatham divisions from 1830 to 1920 and this includes the births and deaths of children of the men. Apart from the usual details, they tell which division a man served in, for example the Royal Marine Artillery. Death registers of those dying at sea from 1893 to 1948 can be found in ADM104/109-142. These give age, rank, place and date of birth and death, cause of death and next of kin. Royal Marine wills from 1786 to 1882 can be seen on Discovery.

Pension records for officers after 1862 and to officers' widows from 1861 can be seen at the TNA in various record series. For officers, try ADM201/22 for surnames from A–M and ADM201/23 for surnames from N–Z. For widows' pensions, see PMG16 for 1836–1870 and PMG20 for 1870–1919. PMG18 has payments to children of deceased officers from 1837 to 1921.

Men from the ranks from 1842 to 1926 can be searched for on Discovery by using the search box ADM159, medals issued from 1793 to 1995 from ADM171 on Ancestry. Marriages and children can be found as per the officers as noted above, and ditto for deaths. Wills from 1786 to 1882 from ADM48 can be searched by name on Discovery. Also found there are attestation rolls and discharges from 1790 to 1925, and description books from 1750 to 1940 (in ADM 157 and 158 respectively). The former can be searched for online but can only be seen on site. The latter must be searched by division then by name. As well as the marriage registers mentioned above there are at TNA, Woolwich 1822–69, and Portsmouth 1869–81, and Royal Marine Artillery marriage and baptism registers from 1810 to 1923, with gaps.

Soldiers and sailors who fought in particularly famous conflicts were often given grand funerals and significant obituaries in the local press, even if of relatively humble rank. Frederick Hitch, later a cab driver, died in Chiswick in 1913 and, following his burial, was given a very large memorial in the churchyard with a great deal of text on it. He had fought at Rorke's Drift and won a VC. Benjamin Soley, a road sweeper employed by Ealing council, was given a grand funeral on his death in 1906. Although not decorated for gallantry he had been one of the lancers in the Charge of the Light Brigade. On a similar note, when the film *The Four Feathers*, depicting the Omdurman campaign of 1896, was shown in 1939 at a Southall cinema, three veterans from the campaign were honoured guests of the management, and sometimes veterans of campaigns spoke at public meetings about their experiences, often years or decades later.

There are record societies which cater for the army and navy which reproduce contemporary documents and are well indexed by names of those mentioned therein. The Army Record Society is fairly recently established (1984) but there are two volumes covering the Crimean war, two on Indian matters and two on African campaigns. These are made up of letters, one of Lord Roberts' and another of Wolesley's but refer to many other officers and since they are indexed may well be worth a look. The Navy Record Society began in 1893 and had produced many volumes, some covering the Victorian era. The National Maritime

Museum in Greenwich is one of several places which holds copies.

Volunteer Forces

These were the men who were occasional, part-time soldiers who were potentially useful for the defence of the country against any invader; some had previously served in the regulars or were later to do so. The county militia, under the aegis of the lord lieutenant of the county, was the traditional method of defence which had existed from Tudor times, with revisions in 1662 and 1757 and still existed into the Victorian era.

Records of the militia are held partly in the county record offices, which usually give listings of name and parish for the militia in any particular year. They are also listed in the WO17 series at TNA, but these records only list the name of the militia man. Not all counties sent listings to TNA and there is a great diversity of the militia archives in the county record offices. For example, there are no archives of men for the Somerset Militia after 1837 in the county record office or TNA. On the other hand, the Kent History and Library Centre at Maidstone has listings for the West Kent Militia (1852–1858), the East Kent Militia (1852–1860), the Kent Artillery Regiment of Militia (1853–1858), the Kent Yeoman Cavalry (1843–1847) and the Kent Rifle Volunteer Corps (1860–1870). TNA have the returns for the East and West Kent Militia Regiments from 1780 to 1876 and the Kent Artillery 1853–76.

Service records of militia officers from 1764 to 1914 are held in WO76 and can be searched on Discovery by name of man or regiment. Details are limited to name, rank, date of commission and occupation, as in the case of John Henry Gould, gentleman, appointed as an ensign to the Dorset Militia on 14 June 1843. Annual militia lists of officers can be seen in volumes at the TNA library and appointments are listed in *The London Gazette*. The *Army Lists* also list militia officers regiment by regiment, with name, rank and date of appointment.

In 1859 the Rifle Movement was founded because of invasion scares about a possible resurgent French Empire of Napoleon III. Companies of volunteers were formed throughout the country. They trained as marksmen and held social events. Initially most of the men were well to do, as volunteers had to supply their own weapons and uniforms.

Men who served in the militia in Scotland, Wales and Ireland can be traced on Ancestry for the years 1800–1915, which searches the attestation papers. One example is Donald Cameron, born in 1872 in Glasgow, who enlisted in the 25th Regiment of Foot on 9 December 1896.

Local repositories have those records which survive of these men. Local newspapers are also a good source of information about their activities and these usually list officers and those men who gain distinctions, such as winning marksmanship competitions. Derbyshire Record Office have a list of men willing to enlist in the proposed Clay Cross Volunteer Corps (ref. D37/MF/137/2).

Then there were the Imperial Yeomanry, who saw service in the second Anglo-Boer war of 1899–1902. This was a force of volunteer soldiers, cavalrymen, who served in South Africa for the duration of the war only. Readers of *The Blanched Soldier*, a Sherlock Holmes story from *The Casebook of Sherlock Holmes*, includes two such men. Names of men, with place and year of birth, time and place of enlistment and normal occupation were listed on the short term attestation service records. These can be searched for on Ancestry. William Norman Greenwood was one such man, born in Ingleton, Yorkshire, in 1873. He enlisted in the City of London on 30 January 1900. He was a gentleman and was in the special corps. A local newspaper covered his return home and the ball given in his honour.

Chapter 6

LAW AND ORDER

As always, crime was a major concern in the Victorian period, though most readers may know this through the stories of Charles Dickens and Conan Doyle, as well as through a few high profile cases the the Jack the Ripper murders of 1888. The system of courts in this era was not much different from previous centuries, but punishments and detection did change. Some offences at this period, and up to the 1960s, are no longer criminal offences, such as suicide and homosexual acts between men (the latter ceased to be a capital offence in the Victorian era). There are a variety of sources for those enmeshed in the criminal justice system.

Police

Although the Metropolitan Police had been established in London in 1829, county forces were established throughout Britain in the early Victorian era. The 1838 Police Act allowed counties and boroughs to form their own forces, paid for out of the rates and overseen by Watch committees made up of magistrates and others. It was in 1856 that police forces throughout the country were made obligatory and a great number of forces of very diverse sizes, were created.

Their importance as far as this book is concerned, is that these bodies began to keep records. Officers' careers have already been discussed in Chapter 3 and here it is their work that is of importance. Much policing is, of course, very routine and the arrest of the bulk of criminals will only be noted in the press and in the courts.

However, for serious offences, such as murder, treason and so forth, far more work, time and manpower are required. Files on such cases exist (for the Metropolitan Police these are in series MEPO3) and these will include witness statements from the suspects and others, and by or about the victim(s). There is usually a report by the investigating officer. There might also be reports by other officers involved in the case. There may be letters from the public about the investigation and possible suspects and solutions. Medical reports may also be included.

Victims found by police, 1893. *(Author's copy of* The Strand *Magazine, 1893)*

Police archives may be held in the county record office for the district where the force was. They can also be found with county police museums, as is the case in Chelmsford for Essex. The Metropolitan Police files at TNA do include material about cases which occurred elsewhere, as well as in Greater London. This is because the Met established a detective force, which many of the smaller forces lacked, and the county chief constables sometimes called in their help. Thus the infamous Road House Murder of 1860, which happened in Wiltshire, led to Detective Inspector Jonathan Whicher being sent from London to try and ascertain the killer of 3-year-old Francis Saville Kent. There is also a small file on the 1870 Denham (Buckinghamshire) massacre held at TNA. However, some county record offices do not have files concerning police investigations. The amount of existing information varies considerably, from a few pages in one file to there being numerous files.

The criminal courts

There were a number of criminal courts. The lower courts were overseen by magistrates and dealt with the vast majority of cases (the fictional Oliver Twist appears before such a court for pickpocketing). These courts usually dealt with the lesser offences in which the sentence given was generally more limited. They are the petty sessions. Magistrates or justices of the peace were not professional lawyers but were often gentlemen or clergy of the county. Those accused rarely had long to wait for summary justice to be dealt out – or an acquittal if there was deemed want of evidence provided by the witnesses called. Sentences were either custodial, or a fine. More serious offenders could not be sentenced at these courts but had to go through them before being sent to the county gaol as a prelude to the assizes courts.

There are also the Quarter Session court records for the counties in England and Wales. These can be seen in the appropriate county record office. In some instances they have been digitised. At Essex Record Office, for example indictments and calendars of prisoners can be seen free via the office website, though the viewer must be registered with an ARA card.

The archives of these courts are held at the county record office in question. Court registers list, in chronological order, the cases held before the magistrates, giving the name of the defendant, the crime for which they were charged, the verdict and the sentence. There are usually no indexes for names, so unless an approximate date is known, searching for an individual can be a long task. Several cases are normally held each day.

Some trial papers can be seen on Ancestry and these include for this period the England and Wales criminal registers from 1791 to 1892. These give basic details of name of defendant, year of birth, charge, date and place of trial and verdict. An example is Richard Harper, born in about 1813, charged with housebreaking at Middlesex on 11 May 1840. He was acquitted.

For the 'lesser' criminal courts in Scotland, who maintained their independent legal system as a condition of the Act of Union of 1707, in this period there are the lower courts of the justices of the peace in quarter sessions and the sheriffs' courts (from 1870 there were fifteen of these) and who also deal with civil cases as well as criminal ones. The majority of the records of the latter, which include criminal registers and court books, indictments and lists of juries, are held at the National Records of Scotland (NRS). Quarter sessions records are split, with some at the NRS and some at county level. For other jurisdictions, court archives are held locally, such as in Jersey, the Isle of Man and so on.

A better source, though an incomplete one, for hearings at magistrates' courts, is the local press, who usually give more details, but only have space for a handful of cases. *The Buckinghamshire Advertiser* for 24 July 1866 reported numerous hearings from the county petty sessions. A couple were as follows:

A PUGILISTIC HONEYMOON

George Finch, a woodcutter in the employ of Thomas Truesdale Clarke, Esq., of Swakeleys, Ickenham, was summoned for having assaulted his wife.

It appeared that the parties had been married only five weeks, and that a fight brought the nuptial day to a close. One day he threatened to chop her down with a bill-hook.

Margaret Finch deposed that at the time in question he took her by the throat, and dragged her across the room, and bruised her arm, at the same time threatening to throw her into a pond and drown her, and she was afraid he would do so. She made this complaint without malice or ill-will.

Mrs Randall, who heard the disturbance, also heard the husband say, 'Don't spit in my face', and the complainant, who was clapping her hands and dancing exasperatingly, rejoined, 'You hit me, you b—'. The defendant was a quiet man, but the complainant was an offensive female.

The defendant was required to enter into a bond in the sum of £5 to keep the peace for one calendar month.

ABANDONED ASSAULT SUMMONS

David Blackwell attended in answer to an assault summons preferred against him by Charlotte Guy. Mr T.F. Jennings, solicitor, of New Hillingdon, appeared to conduct the case for the defence, and said that he

> believed the defendant, who was not in attendance, was ashamed to appear. The case was dismissed.

The higher courts were the assize courts, which dealt with the most serious crimes and for which the death sentence could be awarded. By 1837 the number of crimes for which sentence could be given were vastly reduced compared to the previous era. The country was divided into a number of assize circuits; six in England and Wales (previously dealt with – alongside Chester – by the Court of Great Sessions until the 1830s), made up of adjacent counties, except for that of Middlesex, which included London.

For the minority of serious offences, such as murder and treason, defendants were tried at the county assizes by a judge and jury, with a prosecuting barrister for the Crown and a barrister for the defence for defendants were then not allowed to speak in their own defence except to give a plea at the onset. Assize courts were heard in the county hall in the county town (Lewes in the case of Sussex, for example) twice a year and so defendants could be waiting in prison for several months before their case was heard. Capital sentences had fallen dramatically in the early nineteenth century but there remained several which carried the ultimate penalty of death.

Assize archives are held at TNA. They can be searched for on TNA's Discovery site by name of defendant, and file contents mostly contain miscellaneous papers associated with the trial rather than a transcript of the trial itself. For Scotland there is the High Court of Justiciary in Edinburgh, which was also a touring court, as with the assize judges in England and Wales. Their archives are held at the NRS. There are several series of records held. First, there is series JC26, which is the copy of indictment, witness depositions, confession and other evidence. Summaries of proceedings are in class JC6-9 for cases heard in Edinburgh and for the circuit cases, JC10-14. Some trial transcripts from 1868 can

Dr Neill Cream. *(Wikicommons)*

be found in JC36; summaries of trial proceedings are in JC2-5; for circuit cases these exist from 1890 in JC15. The Lord Advocate's department is another crucial figure in Scotland's judicial system. Records AD14-15 include pre-recognition documents. These are written statements provided as evidence by witnesses which may not necessarily be called as witnesses at the trial but which do contain personal information about those involved in the case. Even if there was no trial these statements still exist and are worth checking.

The exception to this is the Old Bailey trial proceedings from 1678 to 1913, which can be viewed online for free, at Oldbaileyonline. This can be searched by almost any term wished; defendant, victim, location, crime or witness. It gives an account of the trials with statements by all concerned and the verdict. Some are merely a few sentences and some are several pages long. One relatively short example is as below:

> On 22 June 1885 one Herbert Stanley, aged 17, was on trial, accused of the theft of 160 boxes of cigarette papers.
>
> ROBERT MILLER. I am warehouseman at Crossbills, Roche, and Co., of 56, Carter Lane—on 22nd May the prisoner came and said, 'I have come from Mr. Barber, of Dalston, for 100 boxes of cigarette papers; I will take 50 with me, and call or send for the other 50 to-morrow'—I showed him a case conteining [*sic*] 160—he said 'That will do; can it be taken in a cab?'—he got a cab—I assisted him, and he took them away—he signed for them, 'H. Stanley'—this box (*produced*) is similar to them.
>
> *Cross-examined.* I am quite sure you are the person—I picked you out from two others on Islington Green—no one pointed you out.
>
> EDWARD BARBER. I am an agent and traveller, of 1, Bloomfield Street, Dalston, and am a customer of Mr Miller—I do not know the prisoner—I did not authorise him to obtain these cigarette papers—he never delivered them to me.
>
> ROLAND BIGNELL. I am a tobacconist, of 183, Upper Street, Islington—on 30th May the prisoner offered me 100 boxes of cigarette papers similar to this—I bought five of them.
>
> BERESFORD THOMAS FOYLE. I am a tobacconist, of 37, Houndsditch—I bought some cigarette papers similar to this, not of the prisoner—on one occasion the prisoner was with the man, but took no part in the deal—I have

bought several times of the man for six months—my first deal with him was in February—I bought one parcel on 23rd May—the man was alone then—I keep no books—I pay ready money—I give job prices—this is the receipt.

WILLIAM PALMER (*City Detective* 464). On 9th June I was with Miller, who pointed out the prisoner to me with two other young men on Islington Green—I said to him 'I am a police officer; you will be charged with obtaining cigarette papers on 22nd May from 56, Carter Lane'—he made no answer—going to the station I said 'You understand the charge made against you, because you have made no answer to it'—he said 'Oh, I know nothing about it'—he was charged at the station, and gave his name but no address—I found this packet of cigarette papers in his pocket.

Prisoner's Defence. On 28th May I bought 15 boxes of cigarette papers of a man in Kentish Town, and sold them at different places. I made 10*s*. profit, and on it being known to the tobacconist he pointed me out.

ROBERT MILLER (*Re-examined*). I saw him sign the book—I had never seen him before.

GUILTY.— *Six Months' Hard Labour.*

Some – twenty in all – trials can be read in the *Notable British Trials* series which were published in the early twentieth century. These include a transcript of what was said in court by both lawyers and witnesses and include additional material in appendices as well as an introduction to the case. The trials covered are often for murder, such as in the case of multiple poisoners, doctors Palmer and Pritchard. A few of these volumes can be viewed online. It should be noted that though these books are easily accessible the contents should not be seen as 100 per cent reliable. Where the original transcripts of the trials exist, as taken down by shorthand writers present in court, and compared to the NBT version, it will be found that occasionally questions and answers are conflated, a word or two may be omitted, though this does not detract from the overall verity of the NBT. Some court records can be found at FindMyPast; covering Sheffield from 1737 to 1938, York from 1739 to 1851 and Scotland.

If a defendant was found guilty, what then? There were several options, depending on the severity of the crime. Hanging was rare, but in the early decades of our period, transportation was a possibility, though later in the century a custodial sentence was more common.

Executions took place in public until 1868, when the last one took place, of Michael Barrett, in London, for having caused multiple deaths by using explosives to try and rescue his comrades from Clerkenwell Prison. Thereafter they took place in prisons, witnessed by only a handful of staff.

Public executions were very popular entertainment (that of the killers of Christina Collins took place in Stafford in 1840 and the crowd was estimated at being greater than the town's population) and were widely reported in the press. They often comment on the demeanour of the men about to be hanged, a description of them and their last words, if any. They also led to tracts being published and sold at these events and some of these have survived in the British Library and county record offices. They were meant to be educational and moralising. One that appeared in the aftermath of the said Christina Collins case was as follows:

Good Christian people, pray attend
Whilst I relate to you
Concerning of a murder foul
It is, alas, too true.

A helpless female, much beloved
Was travelling to her home,
Three boatmen seized her as she sat,
The water was her home

A letter she had just received
From her beloved friend,
It was her husband, you shall hear
That did for her then send

Upon the water she did go
It was the nearest way,
But sad to tell she never more
Did see the light of day.

James Owen then did her affright
The wretched woman cried,
Dobell said "Tis all in vain,
All help is denied".

Ellis he then assisted them,
They bruised her body sore,
Their hearts never did once relent
Till life it was no more

'Twas on the 17th day of June
This murder it was done.
They did complete the awful deed
Before the rising sun.

Loud was her shrieks, but all was vain
She all her strength did try,
To save her life she struggled long,
But now she was to die.

Her voice grew faint, life's ebbing stream
Did flow upon the boat,
The glassy eye convinced them all
That they the deed had wrought

They threw the body overboard
To hide the crime they'd done,
But Providence did so ordain
The body should be found.

In Staffordshire these monsters were,
In Rugeley, you shall hear,
They now in prison lie condemned,
Their sentence is passed here.

Christina Collins lost her life
By their most ruthless hand,
May God prepare them all in time
To meet His right hand.

After 1868 information about those hanged is less sure, as only staff were present at the majority of executions in prisons. Newspapers may still have reported these occasions and there may be relevant information in the PCOM files at TNA (searchable by name of the hanged). However, the majority of those found guilty and sentenced to death were not in fact hanged but transported or imprisoned, depending on date.

Transportation

Sending convicted criminals overseas to either the colonies in America or Australia had occurred since the seventeenth century. After 1775 America was no longer an option but in the Victorian era Australia was still used as a destination for convicts. From 1788 to 1867 about 162,000–170,000 people were sent to Australia. This was seen as a more merciful punishment than the capital sentences that would have otherwise have been applicable, but as the Victorian era progressed, colonies were less accommodating to having convicts dumped on their shores and so this option was in decline and ended completely in 1868. Those colonies receiving convicts in the Victorian era were New South Wales until 1840, Tasmania until 1853 and Western Australia from 1850 until 1868. Some were given life sentences and some several years, usually seven or fourteen, but many people stayed to make a new life for themselves.

There are numerous archives pertaining to transportation. Listings of those sent from Britain on the prison ships from 1791 to 1868 can be easily found. Name, where and when convicted, vessels' name, date of departure, colony of destination and term of imprisonment are relatively easily discernible. They can be searched for by name on Ancestry. TNA's website allows descriptions of convicts to be searched for, not by name but by ship, by downloading images from HO11.

There are also records, now at TNA, made from 1858 to 1867 by the ship's surgeon, of patients treated and he normally recorded their name and level of education. This is in MT32 and is organised by ship and date. ADM101 are journals written by surgeons, organised by ship, which give comments on men treated by the surgeons. These can all be seen on Discovery.

Once in Australia, a convict's arrival and fate were documented. Muster rolls for those in New South Wales and Tasmania exist. These can be seen via Discovery, for New South Wales since 1788 and for Tasmania from 1846.

Lists of convicts are to be found in HO10 and can be searched for in Discovery, again not by name but by reading through the images that can be downloaded here. The information provided are sentence, pardon and future employment.

Australia itself has much information about the convicts in a variety of sources. The archives council of Tasmania holds material from 1804, including indents and descriptions. Some of this has been digitised. The Female convicts research centre has material about the women arriving there and their subsequent lives. The Convicts' records website is another source about those arriving and can be searched by name to give dates of arrival and sentence. The Australian Dictionary of National Biography gives information about convicts who later made good and the digitised Australian newspaper site TROVE is another useful source.

It should be noted that prison sentences were more common in the Victorian era than ever before. The decline and ending of transportation meant that this was inevitable. Hitherto, prisons were primarily there to hold prisoners either prior to trial or prior to punishment by death or transportation, or for debtors. Purpose-built prisons were constructed to replace the existing buildings.

This led to the creation of prison registers which listed prisoners. These registers listed the prisoner's name and occupation, a brief description, the length of sentence and date of arrival at the prison and their departure; possibly to another prison. They are arranged in chronological order by the entry of each convict, so unless a date is known, searching can be lengthy. However, if the date of the court hearing or trial which led them to this sentence is known, then the prisoner should have arrived on the same day. They will note if a prisoner was transferred to another prison and also the date of discharge. Most prisoners were given remission for good behaviour, so a six month sentence might well last only five. Prison registers are usually held at the county record office where the prison is located. Some are still held at the prison, as is the case with those for Pentonville and Brixton.

A number of prison registers can be seen on Ancestry and some on FindMyPast (Manchester, 1847–1881, Plymouth 1832–1919 and for Guernsey).

There are also registers of 'criminal lunatics' available to search on Ancestry. These cover 1841–1921. One such man recorded here is John Evans, aged 21, who was admitted in 1867 from a court in Middlesex. His sentence of ten years for housebreaking was passed on 7 January 1867 and he was admitted into an asylum on 7 May 1867. The principal destination for those committing crimes but found to be 'unsane' was Broadmoor, in Berkshire and opened in 1863. Archives for patients in the Victorian period can be viewed at the Royal Berkshire Record Office. It took male and female prisoners.

Not all was necessarily as black as these punishments suggest. There were often petitions for clemency, often asking for a reduction in the sentence, sent to the Home Secretary on the prisoner's behalf, or more likely on the behalf of their family (the Court of Criminal Appeal was not then established). They were often sent by the notables of the locality where the miscreants lived. These petitions would often discuss the prisoner's family, their life and why they ought to be shown mercy, and so a great deal of biographical information is given. Naturally this is to show him or her in the best possible light and to highlight any mitigating circumstances that would help them.

Sometimes the quality of the witnesses against the defendant was attacked. Joseph Orgill, the key witness in a Staffordshire trial against three boatmen for murder in 1840, was deemed remarkably suspect by a number of men in early April 1840. According to William Atkins of Burton upon Trent, a 45-year-old butcher of the High Street, 'he is well acquainted with Joseph Orgill', who had 'defrauded this examinant upon a great many instances to a great extent and used great art and deceit in doing so', as he employed him several times in the last three years. He added, 'as to his general conduct and character he would not give credit to his testimony nor would he believe him on his oath'.

Archives for such from 1819 to 1886 are held in the Home Office (HO) files at TNA in HO17-HO19 and can be searched online. There was also the court for the consideration of Crown cases, formed in 1848, which could quash convictions. Surviving records can be found in the order books for 1853–1859 (KB31) in and the pleadings for 1848–1888 in KB30 but the latter do not give the outcome of the courts. They are arranged chronologically and there are no name indexes, nor can they be searched online.

Some notorious criminal cases have books written about them, as in the case of Dr Thomas Neill Cream, a serial poisoner active in the early 1890s or there may be chapters about such cases in books such as the *Foul deeds and Suspicious Deaths* series which covers particular towns, cities and counties and are published by Pen and Sword. These are secondary sources and some are very well researched and sourced but others are less reliable. They tend to deal with the minority of the most heinous or newsworthy of offences, but should provide matter which can lead to further research.

Old Prison chapel, Lincoln Prison. *(Paul Lang's postcard)*

Old Dungeons, Tolhouse Hall, Great Yarmouth. *(Paul Lang's postcard)*

Social unrest

Compared to earlier centuries – and compared to elsewhere in the world – it can be argued that internally the country was far more peaceful; there were no civil wars, revolutions or invasions. However, there were times of discontent. There was the largely peaceful Chartist movement of the 1840s, strikes at the end of the period and a number of riots. These could be political, such as the Hyde Park reform riots of the 1860s and the Fenian terrorism in 1867 and the 1880s. They could be over poverty and unemployment, such as the Trafalgar Square demonstration in 1887 which turned violent, or over religion. From the point of view of the law, any involving violence were termed criminal and thus the archives and other sources listed above can prove useful.

Finally, we should not forget the victims of crime. Those who are murdered, assaulted or stolen from tend to be under-recorded as the courts and punishment focus on the offender. Newspaper reports usually tell a little about the victim and that may be all there is that specifically relates to them. However, in the rare instances where personal papers survive, the victim's story may appear. When May Larson went through the journals of John Allan Brown (1832–1903), gentleman of Clerkenwell and Ealing, she found a couple of instances where Brown was attacked in the street in the 1860s and he records his unfortunate experiences. Another researcher, Lindsay Siviter, found in a letter to Brown by his brother in 1888, a note about his brother writing to tell how his wife was very distressed by two recent murders in Whitechapel (he advised her to play the piano to distract herself). Evidence that victims of crime are not just those directly affected but those in the wider world as well. Sometimes poor people affected by crime are noted as being helped financially by subscriptions to the relief of themselves or their families, organised by a local notable, perhaps a clergyman or businessman. These are often recorded in the local press and often list subscribers/ donors.

Civil Courts

Many of those who came before the courts did so voluntarily and took recourse to the civil courts in disputes over property, rights and money. Readers of *Bleak House* will recall the interminable Jarndyce vs Jarndyce case; civil cases are referenced in Holmes stories *The Hound of the Baskervilles* and *The Reigate Squires*. There were a number of courts dealing with civil matters.

Up to 1875 the Court of Chancery dealt with equity cases involving disputes over inheritance land, marriage and debts. They were used by people from all walks of life but many did not go all the way to a formal court proceeding. The initial step was the pleadings by all the parties and this can be a fruitful source of information about people's lives and activities. They set out the nature of the complaint, the defendant's reply and the plaintiff's response. Records are held in C2-C18 at TNA, and can be searched for by names of the parties involved.

The case may then continue to the level of depositions and affidavits, where more substantial information about the case is obtained. The records here are divided as to whether the case was held in London or elsewhere. In the former case the records are in series C24 up to 1853, then from 1854 to 1880 in C15-16 and J24. Outside London they are in C11-14. They have to be searched by the name of the suit, not by plaintiff or defendant. Affidavits are at C31 and C41, up to 1875, and at J4 for 1876–1880.

Entry books of court decrees from 1544 to 1875 are in C33. There are contemporary annual indexes to these and these can be viewed at TNA's library.

Next, the judge would appoint the Masters in Chancery to make further investigations into the case. The masters would make their reports and both parties could then respond to these in writing. Masters' documents are searched for by the name of the master not by plaintiff or defendant. To find a master's name you can search the final decrees and orders to see which master was appointed to the case that you wish to investigate. The main series of reports for 1801–1875 are in C38, with other documents in C39-40.

For other masters' documents, the series is split into those before 1852, to be found in C117-126. After 1852 they are held at J23-47, 63-64 and 66-68. To find them you need to know the master's name. For the earlier period, once a name has been established the next step is to consult paper documents C103 in the large document reading room on the second floor of TNA to find which C series covers that master, and then use the contemporary indexes which can be found in the same room to ascertain the document reference number.

Final decrees and orders, if the case goes this far, are to be found at C78 and C79, up to 1903. These are probably easiest to see online at the Anglo-American legal tradition website, aalt.law.uh.edu. Cases settled out of court only exist up to 1844 and can be found at C38 and 44 (the latter is not indexed).

Chapter 7

POVERTY, HEALTH AND DISEASE

There has always been some provision for the needy, whether by the church, state or private individuals acting in concert. All three continued to act thus in the nineteenth century. Ancestors may well appear listed in a workhouse, almshouse, asylum or hospital on the census returns, in which case the institution will be known and then can be investigated for further information (though for some asylums only the initials of the individual are given in census returns). Likewise, death and birth certificates can record someone being born or dying in such an institution. However, it is quite possible that they may have been there at other times, as shall be seen in some of the records which can be seen online, so speculative searches may be useful.

These archives will give some of the medical history of our ancestors as well as the times when they were economically, physically or mentally at rock bottom. It is worth finding the nearest hospitals and other institutions to where they lived in order to check what archives exist for them and whether ancestors darkened their doors, why and when. It is necessary to know what archives exist for the area in which your ancestors lived and try some speculative searches.

They may not exist and they may not refer to your ancestors – but on the other hand you may find something.

It is worth noting that most of the archives discussed below will contain information about people drawn from the working classes. Middle-class people would have paid for private doctors for treatments rather than have gone to general hospitals, or have been sent to private asylums. Records for these do not exist in much quantity. So being poor in this instance is of benefit to the pauper's descendants though not themselves.

Poor Law Unions and workhouses

In 1834 the New Poor Law – strictly, the Poor Law Amendment Act – came into force, which divided England and Wales into about 600 poor law unions, replacing the former parish structure for the care of the needy. Each union was made up of a number of parishes centred on a market town for administrative convenience (and so could cross county boundaries) and resulted in the building of a workhouse in order to house those who were to be relieved; by 1841 about 320 had been built (many already existed but were usually very small). They were financed from the poor rates from the parish, as had been the case under the Old Poor Law. Administration was by an elected Board of Guardians who met regularly and who employed a master and mistress. Inmates were fed and sheltered but were given work to do if they were able bodied. Numbers of paupers housed in this way rose from 123,004 in 1850, to 215,377 in 1900. Workhouses varied in their size; some housed under 100 people and others several hundred. It should be added that these were highly controversial, with opposition from both Tories and Radicals; it led to serious unrest in Wales in what became known as the Rebecca riots.

Most of those housed included the very young, the very old and the disabled. Sometimes their residence was very temporary, in response to a domestic emergency. However, outdoor relief still occurred in some cases.

Admission and discharge books are the main source of archives of use to the family historian as these will provide details of all those who entered therein. Similarly, in some cases there may be indoor relief books. Date of admission and discharge are given, the name and age of the individual with parish and occupation if any. Some asylums took photographs of the inmates, either as individuals or in groups engaged in therapeutic activities, and many of these still survive.

Some relevant archives can be found on Ancestry. A couple of examples from Swansea workhouse are Ellen Swan, of 33 Western Street, who was given 3*s* per week outdoor relief. Elizabeth Davies of Castle Walls, aged 61 and suffering from bronchitis, was awarded 2*s* 5*d* per week. Others can be found on FindMyPast, such as those for Wakefield from 1700 to 1915; for Manchester, 1800–1911; Norfolk, 1796–1900; and Sheffield, 1720–1915.

Admission and discharge registers do not always survive. However, there are other sources for workhouse inmates. Creed registers are another useful source from 1869, when the Christian denomination had to be recorded for each inmate. These are listings of inmates, birth date, next of kin, denomination, parish of admission, date of admission, reason for admission and discharge or death. For children under 12 the parent's religion was recorded here. Arranged chronologically, few seem to have been digitised. Birth and death registers for workhouses may also exist.

Less often, there are punishment books detailing those who broke the rules, listing in what way and when, and the punishment inflicted and when. There may also be additional comments by the guardians about the inmate, the offence and the punishment. Most of those who broke the rules were men.

Minute books of the guardians' meetings may refer to individuals if there was a strong reason for them to be mentioned, but as with school log books they are probably a better source of information for staff not patients. Staff registers, where they survive, are another source of information as to who worked there, when they were employed and when they left, their pay and other remarks. Generally speaking it is the minute books of the union administrators which exist in their entirety.

Correspondence from the workhouses can be found at TNA in series HO45 and HO144 which cover 1839–1979 and 1868–1959 respectively. There is also the correspondence in HO46/1-133, covering 1839–1901. These may refer to individual inmates and should give an indication of noteworthy matters which occurred at particular workhouses. They are not the family historian's first port of call, however.

Despite the workhouses, many parishes continued to give outdoor relief, either in money payments or in goods such as food, clothing or fuel. These should be noted in the appropriate parish vestry minute books and overseers' archives. Most records for workhouses are held at the county record office; some record offices will hold them for more than one poor law union.

Almshouses

These were charitable foundations funded by money from a wealthy individual and were usually quite small and catered for only a relatively few individuals. Entry was restricted by age, often by having lived long in a locality and by being of good character. They provided accommodation with food and fuel and often a small pension. Some were founded in the seventeenth century but were refounded and rebuilt in the nineteenth century, and some were of, what was then, modern origin. They were usually run by honorary trustees, often as an adjunct of the parish vestry, but sometimes could be run by other organisations such as the Goldsmiths' Company who had an almshouse in Acton. The York Merchant Adventurers' Company also financed an almshouse in that city.

Most of the inmates were women because of their longevity, and often widows. They were not allowed to accept public monies, however.

Relevant archives should be held with the organisation which administered these. County record offices usually hold almshouses archives and these often include registers of applicants and registers of inmates, usually arranged alphabetically. In some cases there are records of the petitions drawn up by applicants or those acting on their behalf, stating why such a person should obtain a place there. These

Iver Almshouses. *(Author's photograph, 2025)*

Woolaston Almshouses, Highgate. *(Paul Lang's postcard)*

give a unique insight into that person's social and economic condition at that time.

The St Stephen's almshouses in Ealing had to elect almspeople by committee. The choice in 1898 fell on:

> George and Mary Marshman, who have lived in St Stephen's parish for 24 years & who are both over 70 years of age now living in Castle-Bar Mews.
>
> Proposed by Mr Tyndale & seconded by Mr Daw. Caroline Ryder, widow, 85 years of age, now living in extreme wretchedness in the cottage attached to Pittshanger Farm, proposed by Mr W.S. Tyndale & seconded by Mr Way.

Two years later Mrs Ryder had died and so an application by one Mr Slatter and his wife was received. They were resident in the parish and had been so for twenty-two years and were employed by Mr Noble of Melbourne Lodge, and were in 'failing health', aged 61 and 62.

Charities

Many wealthy individuals have left bequests in their wills to establish charities. This is usually in the way of giving property or investing money which can provide an income for trustees to administer to achieve the aim of the testator. It may be that the charity is to provide help to needy individuals, such as to help with educational needs or to provide food and fuel to the local poor. Most charities were administered by the parish, by a group of trustees chaired by the vicar, and most parish churches have a memorial board of charities on their walls, listing the benevolent and their charitable aims.

The minutes of trustees should provide information about the charity recipients but in many cases they do not, only that money or, more often, goods in kind, were provided to the deserving.

The distribution book of the charity of Edward Dickinson of Acton from 1857 to 1900 records those whom this charity helped. Dickinson bequeathed £5,000 to be invested in consols yielding 3 per cent annually. It was aimed at the 'labouring, industrious, sober and honest persons' who had married in the past year, and at each Easter listed those nine couples in Acton and Westminster parishes who were to receive £15 each. Recipients of Poor's land rent, another charity, stated the recipient by surname and first initial and whether they were married or not and how many children there were. Another parish had a charity book with lists of each charity and surnames of recipients, with title and initials.

There were also philanthropic societies formed in the nineteenth century. They raised money and used it to alleviate the sufferings of the deserving poor. The society would be administered by a committee who held regular meetings and received requests for help; they would send one or two representatives to the pleader to check their eligibility for assistance in cash or kind. These decisions were then recorded. Their payments were not primarily aimed at those who received poor law payments. The minute books of the Ealing Philanthropic Society reveal that once a new recipient had been identified their full name would be noted in the minute book and then subsequently the minutes would list all those relieved that month, with surname only and amount given; in the 1890s this was £1 each.

Sometimes applications for charities exist. Ealing Dean Allotments were much sought after as a place to grow food. There are a number of application forms surviving. On 28 November 1873 one James Soley, described as a labourer, applied to pay 5 shillings per year in four quarterly payments to have a designated plot. He agreed to pay his rent punctually, not to trespass on other allotments, would keep his in good order and not build anything there. He signed his name at the bottom of the page.

Hospitals

There have been hospitals since the Middle Ages but their numbers increased in the towns and cities in the eighteenth and nineteenth centuries. Some workhouses also had infirmaries attached. Smaller hospitals which emerged in the later nineteenth century were known as cottage hospitals, aimed at people living in the immediate vicinity, rather than having to travel long and potentially injurious distances into a county town or city. Between 1855 and 1898, 294 were established.

South Park, London Hospital. *(Paul Lang's postcard)*

These voluntary hospitals were financed by fees and voluntary subscriptions and payments. In order to encourage these, subscription lists were published in the hospital's annual reports to list those who supported the hospital financially, and with what amount. Doctors working in these hospitals would do so on a part-time basis, as it was unpaid and their services would be noted in the annual reports.

Hospitals were not open to all. It was usual for a would-be patient to need a recommendation from one of the hospital's financial backers. They would have to be granted a ticket of admission by the hospital's governors, setting out the person's name, address and reason for admission; some cases would not be admitted. This led to the creation of such records. Inpatients would have to abide by the hospital's rules, and those not doing so might be banned in future; this led to the creation of 'Black Books'.

Several of these sets of registers are available to see on Ancestry and so can be searched by name. For example there are the London Poor Law Hospital admission and discharge books from 1842 to 1918. One example taken from these is that of Jane Kelly, aged 29 and born in about 1862. She was admitted on 21 September 1891 and lived at 22 Leather Lane Buildings in the City of London. She was described as being married and able bodied. She entered the hospital because she was pregnant and was discharged at her own request on 3 October 1891. FindMyPast also has a number of sets of hospital records; for Northampton General admissions, 1774–1846 and for Derbyshire, admissions and deaths, 1855–1913.

Note that there were also dispensaries in many towns and cities, which were places where the poor could go for medicines and treatment for free. This was dependent on support by those who provided the money for these institutions, and who could nominate people for treatment. Archives can be found in county record offices and some give details of patients. For example, the Kresen Kernow, as the Cornish Record Office has been renamed, has material on the Penzance dispensary patients giving date, name, age, by who recommended and designation, in a series of registers from 1839 to 1884 (X1034/5/26-31).

Archives of hospitals are usually held in the county or borough archives.

Annual reports provided by the hospital committee give a wealth of information, though not about the individual patients themselves. That for Ealing Cottage Hospital in 1895 names the committee members, the hospital staff and a list of about 500 donors, with names and addresses, and the amount they subscribed, ranging from 10*s* 6*d*, as given by Charles Jones to £5 5*s* as given by Sir Spencer Walpole.

Lunatic asylums

Originally it was the poor law who dealt with the mentally ill. An Act of 1808 encouraged the county justices of the peace to establish asylums but this was not obligatory. From 1845 the counties were given the responsibility to care for the mentally ill in their jurisdiction. Some had already done so; in 1829 the justices of the peace for Middlesex had founded a county asylum for London in the parish of Norwood for 300 inmates, but it was expanded throughout the century. These were known as 'pauper' asylums.

The principal archives which deal with patients are similar to those for the workhouses, chiefly the admission and discharge registers and the creed registers. These list inmates, with ages, occupation, date of entry and discharge, if applicable, and cause of admission.

The Middlesex County Asylum archive is held at TLA. There are registers of male and female admissions from 1831; registers of private patients, 1894–1906; registers of criminal lunatics, 1831–1949; discharge books, 1840–1954; registers of discharges, removals and deaths, 1845–1906; autopsy records, 1863–1904, 1892–1967; mechanical restraints, clinical journals, 1854–1873; inquest papers 1861–1872; female casebooks, 1831–1940, and male casebooks, 1845–1942. These are arranged chronologically and are not indexed.

Some admission and discharge registers are accessible on Ancestry. Those of the Fife Asylums from 1860 to 1937 can be searched there. One such patient was Mary Watson, admitted on 11 January 1893. She was 18 years old, single, a mill worker from Lochran, Cleish. She was described as being 'weak' as to her bodily condition. She was apparently suffering from 'mania', with 'organic brain disease with epileptic form of convulsions and chronic bronchitis'. She was discharged on 20 February 1893. Others can be seen on FindMyPast; Prestwich, 1851–1901 and Bethlem 1683–1932.

Many asylums, especially private ones, were small scale with only a handful of patients, often single sex. Dr John Conolly established one at his house in Hanwell in the 1840s. Some were run by women. Many did not last for many years. The private asylums catered for people whose families could pay for them to be here. Directories usually list such places. The majority of these archives have long ceased to exist, but should be searched for by the name of the proprietor. Some records of private asylums can be found in the quarter sessions archives of the appropriate county. The Bethlem Museum of the Mind holds the archives of several institutions and these are detailed at https://en.wikipedia.org/wiki/Bethlem_Museum_of_the_Mind

Friendly societies

In the eighteenth and nineteenth centuries people insured themselves against ill health by joining such a group and paying a regular subscription. Some were for women only, such as the Benthall Female Friendly Society of Shropshire. In return for this they would receive a payout if they were ill. Records of these groups are usually held at the relevant county record office. They often include lists of members, payments they made to the society and any payments they received in times of need and the dates of such. Some provide additional details. For example, the Girls' Friendly Society of Ettington, Warwickshire (held at the county record office for 1875–1892), give information about the girls' employment and character.

Vaccination records

The great killers of the nineteenth century, smallpox, cholera and typhus were combatted by vaccination. Smallpox vaccination was made compulsory by a law passed in 1854. Smallpox vaccination certificates exist to give proof of compliance and these give the name of the child, the father's name, parish and county of abode, and date of vaccination. There is no central register and often these only exist in family papers. Some vaccination registers appear in county record offices, in the collections of the Boards of Guardians, often covering several years. The Kent History

Centre holds registers for the West Ashford Union from 1875 to 1882 and for the Hollingbourne Union from 1876 to 1889. Online at FindMyPast are those for Glasgow from 1801 to 1854, giving the patient's name and address, age and date of vaccination. Ann Fraser, aged 8 months, of 19 Findlay Street, was one, on 31 October 1853.

Chapter 8

LAND AND PROPERTY

Having looked at the fates of some of the poor, we now turn to the more affluent in society, those who were possessed of land and property. These are the basis of wealth and power, then as now. In the Victorian era the number of property owners and small capitalists increased and their earthly possessions can be tracked as records were kept.

Tithe records

The Tithe Commutation Act was passed in 1836 in order to ascertain land ownership and occupation; it was the most significant land survey since the Domesday Book of 1086 and was organised parish by parish in England, Wales and Ireland. A tithe was a tax payable to the church and had been in force for centuries. It was becoming increasingly controversial in the early nineteenth century when the plurality of Christian denominations became more apparent and widespread as already noted.

There are two important records created: maps and apportionments. The maps show the plots of land, each of which is allocated a number, as well as buildings and geographical features. The apportionment is a list of each parcel of land which appears on the map and gives the area in acres, roods and pecks, the land usage – often pasture or meadow in the case of rural districts. Then there is the name of the owner and the name of the occupier. These are not generally indexed, although some local indexes to names of occupiers and owners do exist and so make searching many pages far quicker.

When you find which parish your ancestor was living in in 1841 it is worthwhile checking the tithe apportionment to see whether they are listed as an occupier or owner of land. Not every householder will be there of course. But in some cases an ancestor, especially if well to do, might own several plots of land. Of course some will own land in more than one parish, not just the one they inhabit. Knowing what someone owned and exactly where they lived is useful, for the 1841 census is often quite vague as to where in a parish someone lived, as street addresses in rural parishes are not always given.

Records are held at TNA (IR 29 for the apportionments, IR 30 for the maps), the diocesan archives and with the parish; the latter may well no longer retain them but will have deposited them in the county record office along with other early parish archives. Some tithe records can be seen online; those for Wiltshire are on FindMyPast. These give occupier and owner and brief details of the land in question. One example is that of John Turner, who occupied a house and garden in a backstreet in Warminster which was owned by the Warminster prebend. Genealogist UK also contains copies of these records.

There was also the tithe redemption that took place in the later nineteenth century. This was when a lump sum could be paid to negate the need to pay any further tithes. Certificates were given to those who paid and these should be held in the parish and diocesan archives, giving the name of the payer, the payment and the date. Tithe payments ended in the early twentieth century.

Electoral registers

The Victorian era saw great steps forward to Britan becoming a parliamentary democracy as more and more people were eligible to vote for their MPs and councillors. This is also good news for researchers because it led to more names being recorded. Lists of those eligible to vote are crucial when parliamentary elections are held and listings have been published since the late seventeenth century in what were then known as poll books. However, they were not published unless an election was forthcoming.

In 1832 there had been a major overhaul of the franchise, known as the First, or Great, Reform Act. This radically altered the medieval system of parliamentary constituencies by the creation of new ones in the industrial towns and cities in the Midlands and north of England. Previously towns such as Manchester and Leeds were part of the Lancashire and Yorkshire county constituencies rather than being represented in their own right. However, the act did not lead to a huge rise in the number of those men aged 21 or over and eligible to vote, as there was still a minimum property qualification.

The 1867 and 1884 reform acts led to more changes and increases in the number of men eligible to vote. The first added a million electors and the second another two million, and in both cases there was another redistribution of seats. By 1884 almost all householders could vote if they wished (and after 1871 there was a secret ballot); some lodgers could do so if they paid more than a certain amount of rent. Furthermore, and this is often overlooked, female householders could vote but only in local government elections for councillors, not for MPs. There was certainly a large minority of households headed by women either as widows or as reasonably well off spinsters. There were also instances of multiple voting if an individual was entitled to a vote based on their home address, and also their business address if this was different.

Poll Books of electors were compiled after the elections and list which candidate(s) an elector voted for (constituencies were often represented by two members), so it is possible to learn your ancestors' political affiliations (up to 1871). Of course, it is possible that an elector might vote the way his employer or landlord suggested.

All this resulted in annually produced electoral registers listing the names and addresses of those who could vote. It does not give any other information. The information is organised by constituency and then, for towns and cities, by ward, and then by street address in alphabetical order. You may need to look through several wards to find the ancestor in question. Furthermore, there are, within each ward, further sub categories by owners and tenants and by lodgers. In small villages there is often an alphabetical list of names by parish and by surname.

The section of Chiswick voters in the Middlesex electoral registers from 1890 to 1914 are divided into four parts. The first is an alphabetical list of those eligible to vote in parliamentary elections – men only – by name and then with address. The second list is of those who can only vote in local elections – almost entirely female – in alphabetical order by name. Third is a list of lodgers who are eligible to vote in order by name. Apart from giving an address, there is a description of the rooms occupied, whether furnished or not, and the name and address of the landlord if different from that of the lodger. So we learn that Harry Willshire Hardy and William Frederic Hardy had a room on the first floor, furnished, at High Road, Chiswick, and their landlord was Benjamin Hardy of the same address. Finally there is a list of people who could vote because of their property in Chiswick, but who lived elsewhere; Charles Edward Leyton of 272 Hagley Park, Edgbaston in Birmingham, was one of these. Some electoral registers can be seen online at Ancestry and FindMyPast and can be searched by name. Others are held in the appropriate county or borough record office.

Trade directories

Those readers who are old enough will recall telephone directories which were published annually and list householders and businesses with a BT landline. We'll come to Victorian telephone directories shortly, but more important are the trade and street directories. These have existed in London since the seventeenth century and for other major cities, such as Liverpool, since the eighteenth. But it was the Victorian age that was their zenith.

Basically, directories were commercial listings of householders and businesses in a particular geographical district and would be sold in those districts. *Kelly's* was the predominant producer of these books, but there were others, often short lived, such as *Pigot's*, and some one-offs. *Kelly's* began by publishing directories that covered a number of counties, such as the 1845 directory of Middlesex, Essex and Hertfordshire, but as time and populations progressed, they published single county directories. These would be divided by parish in alphabetical order and after giving general historical and official information (the latter is useful in itself as it lists principal officials for local institutions, civil and religious) then lists in alphabetical order, inhabitants and businesses. In the country town of Abingdon there were thirty-nine 'principal inhabitants', and of these fifteen were women and another five were clergymen; the town's population being just under 10,000. The number listed in the commercial list was far higher.

The first list is of householders, but only what are sometimes termed 'principal inhabitants', usually the middle-class and wealthy residents. Agricultural and industrial workers will not be found here. It will give the addresses of those named. The commercial part of the list will include shopkeepers and other businessmen/women, innkeepers and others such as craftsmen employed in their own right.

Towards the end of the century *Kelly's* also produced local directories, especially for towns and cities which were, in modern terms, far more socially inclusive. These were divided as before, but in the householders' section, pages were divided in alphabetical order by street and then householders were listed by street number, the name of the house was often given as well. There was also an alphabetical list of householders, with addresses, so that makes searching far easier.

The householders are not necessarily the houseowners, but could well be tenants. Note that a house could be tenanted by more than one family and usually only one name is given. Whereas for men the Christian name or its abbreviation (Jo for John or Jas for James etc.) is given, female householders are usually only named by their title, so Mrs or Miss. Directories give no indication as to the size of a household.

These directories focused on more affluent districts, so in London there are few for parishes in London's East End other than the county directories (Middlesex, then London from 1889). Middle-class Lewisham and Blackheath were covered, but not neighbouring working-class Deptford.

Sometimes a person might be listed under both the householders' section and in the commercial section if they had a business in the same locality; or perhaps the business might have been located in another district.

Inclusion in a directory, unlike electoral registers and rate books, was not mandatory. Information for these books was collected in the year prior to that on the directory's title date. So if someone died or moved in December 1889 they could still appear in the directory for 1890.

Beware that house names / numbers may change over time; even street names, so when it seems that there has been a move of address, it may not really have been so. Many houses were known by names not numbers and so a systematic search through directories year by year where they exist, should be undertaken as houses are given numbers. Streets might be sub-divided into terraces or villas and these were later renumbered and the sub-divisions were removed. Or streets might be renamed, especially if small.

Directories can be found for each locality in the appropriate record office or local history library. The Guildhall Library in London has a large collection of directories from throughout the country and there is a smaller collection on the shelves of TNA's library. Some directories from the late eighteenth to the early twentieth centuries can be viewed online at Directoriesonline, where they are divided by county. It is not comprehensive but does include many and so is worth looking at for a start. FindMyPast has a number of directories including those for York from 1781 to 1955, Hampshire 1863–1927, and a number of Scottish directories.

Women are not invisible in these directories but they are less prominent than men. This can be seen in two instances. First, the householder will usually be male. Second, where they are female, probably widows in the cases of 'Mrs', only the surname and title are usually stated, so 'Richardson, Mrs/Miss' never 'Richardson, Agnes'. Third, businesses were often run by men, but a significant number of drapers, inns and schools were run by women.

The first known British telephone directory was published in 1880. It was for 248 people and businesses in London. No telephone numbers were given because it was a case of ringing up the exchange and asking for one of the 248 people or businesses listed. As the years went on, more people and businesses were added to these lists, which still covered London only, but even so, by 1901 telephone use was very limited indeed and very few homes had them. Telephone directories can be searched on Ancestry. There were no provincial telephone directories until 1900 in Britain.

Rate Books

Taxation records are a crucial source of information for family historians. One of the oldest and most universal forms of taxation is that levied by the parish since the sixteenth century: the rates (known as council tax since 1991). This was a tax based on the value of a property, whether domestic or commercial, that was within the boundaries of a said local government district and was set annually, or even bi-annually, by the parish or council to meet their expenditure requirements.

This resulted in listings in book form being created. These were of those who had to pay the rates, with their name, the amount owed and the property to which the payment pertained. In rural districts, as with electoral registers, the only information was the name of payee and the amount; possibly they might be listed by district in the said parish. In towns, the address would usually be given.

In the early Victorian period the rates were set by the parish; they also might be sub-divided into rates for different purposes, usually the poor rate (the highest of all), the highway rate and the church rate and these are usually found in different books, each often covering a number of years. By the later Victorian era when councils were the dominant body in local government, rate books were composed annually and all the rate demands amalgamated into one sum. These books often noted who did not pay up and this could be an interesting insight into an ancestor's finances and lifestyle – and could lead to a court case.

Rate books, as with electoral registers and directories, can help show where someone lived in between the census years and when they moved address. They also indicate how wealthy someone was by the amount of their rate bill, based on property value.

Relatively few rate books have been digitised. They can be viewed at the county or borough record office. They are rarely, if ever, indexed by name. Sometimes records for a particular place can be located in more than one repository. In London parish and some council archives are divided between The

London Archives (TLA) and the borough archives. However, some have been digitised on FindMyPast; including those for Manchester in the nineteenth century, Plymouth and West Devon from 1598 to 1933, Westminster from 1634 to 1900, Southwark, Portsmouth, Ayrshire 1813 to 1846. They provide the name of the owner and occupier, address and rateable value and can be searched by name. Rate books are, of course, useful for finding the name of property owners as well as those living at an address.

The equivalent in Scotland are valuation rolls, from 1855 to 1989. These are held at the NRS under reference VR and are some of the most commonly used archives there. They have been digitised from 1855 to 1957. They are arranged by administrative district and were sent to the Register House in Edinburgh. For each property they give the name and designation of the owner, the tenant's name and the amount payable. For rural districts the address is merely stated as the particular village or hamlet in which the property was located, but more details were listed as time went on.

Blair Atholl Castle, Scotland. *(Author postcard)*

There were numerous other taxes which some of our ancestors – especially those who were property owners – had to pay. There was the Land Tax from 1692 to 1963; the Window Tax up to 1851 (never applied in Scotland) and the house duty thereafter; a horse tax from 1784 to 1874; a tax on male servants from 1777 to 1852; gun tax from 1870 to 1872; and a dog tax from 1796 to 1882. Most of the few surviving tax records are held in the county record offices and are usually listings of names and amounts payable.

Maps

Apart from the incredibly useful tithe maps already discussed, the main types of map are the Ordnance Survey maps. These are very detailed at 1:2500 scale and for some major towns and cities are even more detailed (and for some large buildings even show rooms). They mark buildings (whether domestic, ecclesiastical, public or commercial), streets and other geographical features such as woods, orchards and bridges. For the Victorian period maps were published in 1865 and 1894.

The maps do not in themselves name individuals or families but do provide context to their lives by seeing where they lived, worked and worshipped, and how these districts changed over time. Railways can be shown and industrial premises built. New streets, churches and schools appear.

Many of these maps can be viewed online for free at the National Library of Scotland website. Paper copies can be found at the British Library and also at county and borough record offices and local history libraries for the districts that they cover.

Copies of many of the Victorian OS maps can be bought from the Godfrey maps business, costing £3.50 at time of writing. TNA's book shop sell many of these, as do county and borough record offices for the locality in question.

Some directories often include maps of the locality but unfortunately many of these have been ripped out long before they reached the repository. Where they survive these can be useful in order to fill in the gaps between the OS maps which were published decades apart, though are far less detailed.

Maps can also be produced by other organisations for other purposes. Estate plans of landed estates were produced periodically by the landowner and show what their lands were being used for. These may give more information than the OS maps, showing perhaps where particular workers lived and worked. County records offices may hold these if they are not still at the estate itself.

The Charles Booth poverty maps of London – which actually show all shades of wealth in the late nineteenth century – can be viewed online. Gold denotes riches and Black means desperately poor, with various shades of blues and reds in between. It is limited to the county of London and not Middlesex as a whole. The maps can also be seen in book form.

Deeds are another important form of property documentation as they denote the transfer of property from one party to another. Up to 1925 transactions had to show as many deeds as possible, and not just the last thirty years of title. Most borough and county record offices will have thousands of these. They are usually catalogued by the names of the parties involved and so should be picked up easily from a search of the online catalogue. They enable a researcher to learn what property an ancestor either bought, sold or rented and for how much. There should be a description of the said property and often a basic block plan of it in relation to the locality. There are deeds registries for Middlesex, and for the East, North and West Ridings of Yorkshire, which are organised by name of the person selling the property and cover from the early eighteenth to the early twentieth centuries. They are at TLA and the county record offices for the North and East Ridings, and at Wakefield Archives for the West Riding.

Often deeds are found in collections with several deeds covering the same property over the decades. These are particularly useful for the researcher. Deeds involve many people. First, there is the landowner who sells the land to the builder. Then there is the builder who will buy the land on which he builds the properties. Then there is the person or persons who buy or rent the property. They may then sell or rent it as time goes on, or may have to mortgage it in order to raise the money to buy it. Eventually the property will pass to another.

Abstracts of deeds are a useful shortcut to having to view many deeds. An abstract is a summary document of the deeds to a property, giving parties and dates as a minimum.

For Scotland, land ownership records can be found in the General Registry of Sarsines which consist of 50,000 volumes of land ownership from 1554 onwards. These are held at the NRS.

Insurance policies are another good source for property as householders and businesses sought to have their property protected from disasters. These will provide the name, address and occupation of the person taking out the policy, the date, the premium, the dates of subsequent payments as well as a brief description of the property and its contents. Some major nationwide insurance companies have their archives at TLA which cover up to the 1860s. These are those of the Sun Fire Office, the Royal Exchange and the Hand in Hand. Some are indexed. The Phoenix insurance company papers are at Cambridge University Library and those of the Westminster Fire Office are at Westminster Archives. These insurance companies had national coverage.

Phoenix Insurance Company emblem. *(Author's copy of* The Strand, *1893)*

Estate records

The landed estates which formed the basis of power of many of the wealthiest in the country produced a great many papers as part of their administration. They can include correspondence, maps, surveys, rentals, leases and accounts. These can shed light not only on the landowners but also on their many tenant farmers who rented land from the owner. Many of these archives are in county record offices; for example, the archives of the Dartmouth estate are divided between Leeds Archives and the Staffordshire Record Office, and those of the Grosvenor estate are at Cheshire Archives and at Westminster City Archives, but where the estates are still in existence, some may well be in the hands of the owners and may be accessible to bona fide researchers.

Some rental records are available on Ancestry; namely for Bedfordshire from 1838 to 1929, West Yorkshire from 1380 to 1932, and Griffiths' Valuations between 1847 and 1864, which cover Ireland. They are organised by parish and give the names of landlord and tenant, a very brief description of the property, the parish it is in, acreage, rental and rateable values. A Bedfordshire example is that of Mary R. Bramwell, who occupied Canterbury Villa in Ampthill, a house and grounds of 1 acre, and 13 perches from Henry Bowles Field. It had an annual rental of £40 and a rateable value of £32. There was a national valuation of 1873 of properties of one acre and more, which can be searched in FindMyPast, and gives place and acreage.

Although 1910 is post Victorian, it is probably worth mentioning the Land Values books of that year, sometimes known as the Domesday books. This was the first national survey of property since the tithe investigations of the beginning of our period. Organised by parish they list each property, giving both owner and occupier. This could be useful in working backwards as the information in 1910 might (or might not) be the same as that a decade earlier and so might provide useful information about property owned by your ancestors.

Chapter 9

MIGRATION AND IMMIGRATION

Although population growth in Britain was significant in this period, there was also a large degree of migration, especially from poorer districts. The decline in employment in the countryside for farm workers by 40 per cent between 1861 and 1901 in England and Wales led to emigration by many of these men (not women, as they could easily find employment in domestic service, a growth industry for women at the time). The appeal of possible wealth in America or Australia with the gold rushes led some Britons to emigrate there. Emigration to parts of the growing British Empire for the commercial prospects was another reason for temporary or permanent resettlement abroad. Most of the emigrants were men and this added to the gender imbalance at home; migration of single women was not encouraged.

It has been estimated that about 10 million people migrated from Britain between 1815 and 1930. Even though only about half of these migrated in our period, that still represented a lot of people. They were not limited by social class or profession. Many did not do so permanently; about 40 per cent of English and Welsh migrants between 1861 and 1913 returned (some only intended to go abroad to make money and then return), though most of the Irish leaving during, and in the aftermath of, the Famine remained overseas. In the earlier decades it was common for a whole young family to emigrate, but in the later nineteenth century most migrants were single young men. Some were helped by official schemes; between 1846 and 1869 this numbered 339,000 people, but most paid their own way, which could be one or two month's wages.

Most of the immigration into Britain in the nineteenth century was from elsewhere in Europe. Until 1905 there were no immigration checks or limits, and immigration was often to escape political or religious persecution in countries such as Russia and Germany. Following the failure of the 1848–9 revolutions on the Continent a number of political radicals came to Britain; among them, famously, was Karl Marx. Migration was not always forced; German businessmen arrived in Manchester and Leeds (both major centres of commerce which held out the prospect

SS *Lake Champlain*. *(Paul Lang's postcard)*

of business opportunities for entrepreneurial migrants), and the dockland areas of major cities attracted merchant seamen and labourers of various nationalities. There was a well known Italian quarter in north London, Saffron Hill, noted in the Sherlock Holmes story, *The Adventure of the Six Napoleons*.

Emigration and immigration were not always permanent and some settlers returned after having done exceedingly well, or some might return temporarily to see family members at home.

Later in the century Jews from the Russian empire fled to escape the pogroms. Many settled in the East End of London where Yiddish became one of the most spoken languages. Leeds, Manchester and Glasgow also attracted migrants from Poland and Lithuania. There are a number of Jewish sources for the nineteenth century. The poor Jews' Temporary Shelter was established in the East End and many newly arrived men were met at the docks and offered shelter here. The names of 43,000 men from 1895 to 1914 can be found at http://chrysalis.itsuct.ac.za/shelter/shelter.rtm. Archives of the Jewish soup stall, founded in Spitalfields in 1854, can be seen at TLA. Admission and discharge books for the London Jewish schools should be consulted, as these will give fathers' names and addresses; those for the Jews' Free School for 1791–1999 (4046 and 4290), and the Westminster Jews' Free School 1846–1950 (4047), are at TLA.

Jewish settlers were noticeable in Manchester, Leeds and Glasgow. For Leeds Jews, the following sites are useful: secretlibraryleeds.net/research-collection-guides which has a section on Jewish Leeds. Then there is makorjewishcultureuk.org/heritage and www.jhse.org/branches-1/leeds. The London based *Jewish Chronicle* was established in 1841 and so is another important source. The Scottish Jewish Archives is in Glasgow and includes synagogue minute books, registers and admission lists.

A directory of Jewish businesses in Britain was published in 1894, and this can be searched in FindMyPast. One example from this was M. Kosminski, a wholesale furrier of 48 Berners Street in London. There was a Manchester Naturalisation Society from 1896 to 1909, to which Jewish immigrants wishing to be naturalised contributed a shilling per week and then when enough was raised to apply, one of the subscribers was chosen at random and the process continued. Names of those subscribing and amounts paid and when can be found on FindMyPast.

Some immigration was forced. Percy Savage, recalling his days in the Metropolitan Police, noted that sometimes young women were enticed to London with promises of well paid jobs only to find that they were forced to work in prostitution. Likewise there were stories of young women being beguiled away from Britain with similar offers but ending up in brothels; known as the 'White Slave Trade' – now it would be known as 'Modern Slavery'.

The main sources for immigration from outside Europe are the shipping registers of incoming passengers from 1878 to 1960. These can be searched for by name on Ancestry and are made up of listings of passengers made by the captains of incoming vessels and given over to the Board of Trade. They are made by ship and give basic details of each incoming passenger. The lists will enable you to see if any other family members came with them on that voyage. So one example is that of Mary A. Kosminska, born in 1865, who arrived on the ship *Teutonic*, from New York to Liverpool on July 1894. She was designated as 'a foreigner' aged 29. With her was her 2-year-old son, Mikoli and a younger daughter, Mary Anne.

European arrivals can be traced in Alien Arrivals, covering 1810–1811 and 1826–1869, and the chronologically overlapping Alien Entry Books, 1794–1921. These were returns made to the Home Office. Both can be searched by

The *Majestic*, London to Chicago. *(Author's copy of* The Strand, *1893)*

name on Ancestry. An example from the former is that of Franciscus Liszt, arriving on 16 April 1840 from Hungary. He was described as a composer and stayed two months. His signature appears on the certificate. Alien Entry Books cannot be searched by name but the books themselves have been digitised and can be seen on Ancestry but have to be searched page by page in chronological order so unless you have an approximate idea when someone might have arrived it may be a long search.

There are also the naturalisation certificates from 1870 to 1916. These were for people from overseas who wanted to live permanently and become British subjects. Not all immigrants became naturalised, it should be said. They can be searched for by name on Ancestry and provide some family and biographical details. In the case of Robert S. Medard of Constantinople:

> a subject of the Empire of Austria of the age of 55 years, a correspondence and finance clerk of Her Britannic Majesty's Consulate General at Constantinople is married and has two children under age, residing with him, viz Mary Medard, aged 20 years, Alfred Medard, eleven, and applies to be naturalised.

The certificate was granted on 15 May 1883 and Medard swore the oath of allegiance to the queen.

For outward-bound passengers, the shipping registers for 1890–1960 (accessible on Ancestry) are useful for the later part of our period; again, as with the incoming passengers, they do not exist for ships coming from the Continent. They are arranged by ship and were sent by the captain to the Board of Trade, providing some biographical information on emigrants. An example is that of Andrew Alfred Jones, born in 1873 and described as a labourer. He was sailing on the *New England* from Liverpool on 20 April 1899 and was bound for Boston in America.

The Poor Law authorities assisted poor families to emigrate from 1834 to 1890 with assisted passage to the colonies, where their voyage would be paid for from public money. This was primarily to Australia and it was aimed at providing the new colony with the settlers that they needed there; so any family of bad character would not be helped. Often letters of support would be needed for those wanting to take advantage of this, which provided additional information about them, and references to these – though not the letters themselves – may exist in the Poor Law Union archives for the union in question, in county record offices.

For Scotland, however, from 1845 to 1916 there was a system of passports – not required for anyone else in the United Kingdom prior to the twentieth century. These had to be obtained from the lord provost of either Edinburgh or Glasgow. He recorded the details of those wishing to travel abroad and also to European countries unlike the shipping registers mentioned above.

Those for Edinburgh can be seen and searched on Ancestry. Those for Glasgow are currently only accessible in volumes at the Mitchell Library in Glasgow. An example of the information that can be gleaned from these can be seen from the following example. John Fraser of 3 Golden Acre Terrace, Edinburgh, desired to travel to the Continent and had one F. Grant Ogilvie of Heriot Watt as his reference. He was granted a passport on 19 September 1894. Often the country to which the person was to travel is mentioned explicitly. As the information is organised chronologically it is often possible to see who the person travelled with, perhaps friends or family, and this gives an extra dimension. It might have been a case of students travelling on a tour, for example.

There was also some emigration to South America. In particular Argentina was singled out (think of Poirot's friend Captain Hastings and one of the songs in *Evita*). This began in 1806 but grew as the nineteenth century progressed and families with capital came over to buy land to develop and found banks. Irishmen went over either as farmers or to work on farms, and the Scots established ranches and

Presbyterian churches. There is an online source http://www.argbrit.com which brings together many relevant sources, including church and cemetery records and wills.

The other place in South America to attract significant numbers of Victorian Britons was Patagonia. Between 1865 and 1914 about 3,000 Welsh arrived there, hoping to preserve their language and traditions. Although some stayed on, many others eventually travelled on to New Zealand or Canada. TNA has a passenger list of the first ship to sail there, the *Mimosa* in 1866, at FO118/121. There are also relevant sources at the National Library of Wales.

Otherwise it is a question of checking the archives and newspapers of the country that a person went to. Some of these can be seen on Ancestry, especially the American and Australian ones, and Ancestry has numerous sources for New Zealand, another common destination for Britons in the nineteenth century. There are sources for early settlers, 1840–1864, naturalisation records covering 1843–1981, and a register of ship owners from 1840 to 1950. For settlers, there are electoral registers from 1853 to 2010; cemetery records from 1800 to 2007; school registers from 1850 to 1967; medal rolls for the period 1860–1919; and much more.

For emigrants arriving into America there is also much to find on Ancestry. Some sources are more useful than others. The Irish Immigrant Arrival records from 1846 to 1851 are good for uncovering individual emigrants, such as Patrick O'Reilly for example, born in about 1831, a 20-year-old man who had sailed from Liverpool on the *Columbia*. He was described as a 'workman' and arrived at New York on 1 August 1851. But the system does not allow the viewing of the actual record, so unlike the 1890–1960 shipping registers it does not show with whom he travelled, so any other family members must be searched for individually.

Better are the New York Arrivals, 1820–1957. Searching for an individual, let us say James J. Everard, we not only find that he arrived on 17 June 1897, was born in Cavan, County Meath, Ireland, was a clerk who travelled from Queenstown on the *Awania* and had $26 on his person, but also that he travelled with other family members. We also learn that he was going to stay with his brother, P. Everard, who had already settled there. By 1870 the Irish made up a third of immigrants to America; there were Irish regiments formed on both sides of the American Civil War. Irish emigrants to America after the Famine from 1846 to 1851 can be searched for in FindMyPast. One example was Patrick Mahon, born in about 1823, a labourer, who travelled as a steerage passenger on the *Henry Clay* ship and landed in America on 26 December 1846.

In some cases there may be no substitute for a visit or paying a local records agent to undertake work for you. For example, for British ancestors resident temporarily or otherwise in Barbados, the Barbados Department of Archives, the library of the Barbados Museum, the National Library Service, the university library and the registration department are the key locations for resources. These include electoral registers (from 1867) directories, newspapers, parish registers and notes compiled by previous researchers and an index to plantation owners, though there are no census returns for the nineteenth century.

Although some migrants returned, some did not. There were substantial British communities in India in the nineteenth and twentieth centuries as a result of India being the Jewel in the Crown of the British Empire up to 1947. *The Imperial Kalendar* and the East India and Indian army records have already been mentioned in this book. There are other records, too, of those not in the military or official employment. Indian newspapers for the period can be found on the online British Newspaper Archive: *The Bombay Gazette*, 1792–1868; *The Madras Weekly Mail*, 1876–1908; *India*, 1890–1921; *The Indian Daily News*, 1875–1906; and *The Indian*

Statesman, 1872–1885. Britons in India can also be traced through directories such as the India Directory editions from 1792 to 1859, and the Far Eastern Directories from 1833 to 1941. These can be seen on FindMyPast.

Many missionaries came out from Britain to India and elsewhere in their aim to convert souls to Christianity. There are a number of sources for the missionaries of different denominations who did so. Bengal directories from 1835 list missionaries, as do the Madras dictionaries from this decade. Thacker's *Annual Directory of India* from 1885–1942 lists missionaries of all denominations. Biographies of missionaries up to 1886 can be found in the *Indian Missionary Directory: Memorial Volume*. For more information about individuals and their work, the School of Asian and Oriental Studies Library in London has the archives of the Conference of British Missionary Societies, 1872–1973, and the Commonwealth Missionary Society from 1836 to 1966.

British India postcard. *(Paul Lang's postcard)*

One Rupee. *(Paul Lang's postcard)*

Internal migration was common. Some people did stay in the same location for most of their lives but others did not and the census will show this. In some instances people moved about but little. In the case of Robert Everard, a small farmer and gardener, most of his life was spent in different parts of Lincolnshire. He was born in Leverton in 1853 and by the 1870s was in Glentham. By 1885 he was in Middle Rasen before moving a mile to Market Rasen. In 1891 the family was in Snitterby, 11 miles distant, and then moved to Fairforth by 1893 and then to Clee, a suburb of Grimsby. Flora Violet Munro was born in Edinburgh in 1870 and was employed there as a servant in 1891, but later that decade moved south and was employed in Brighton, Sussex, in 1901. Her move southwards may have been in connection to that of her elder sister who married a jeweller in south London. John Christie was born in Kilmarnock in 1835 but was sent by his father as apprentice in the carpet trade to Kidderminster in 1845, moving to Halifax with his family in

1877 and then retiring to Kidderminster in 1898, where he died in 1917.

All this means that the researcher will need to examine a number of sources, quite possibly held in different locations, to trace the life of their ancestors.

People naturally moved from poorer parts of the country to where there were greater employment opportunities. Rural poverty in the Scottish Highlands and the potato famine in Ireland led many to leave their homeland, either for elsewhere in the world, notably the USA but also to other parts of the British Isles. One naturally thinks of the Irish navvies who did much to build the railways and other hard construction work, though Irishmen were coming to England before 1846 (and many did so in the 1870s and 1880s as a result of the farming depression). They were concentrated initially in London, Lancashire and Glasgow. In 1851, 22 per cent of Liverpool's population were Irish and 13 per cent in Manchester. In 1861 there were 601,634 Irish in England and Wales, and by 1881 there were 218,745 in Scotland. Most were poor and unskilled; in 1881, 82 per cent were day labourers. Catholic archives may be particularly useful in tracking down Irish emigrants.

Anyone whose ancestors emigrated or were immigrants may want to travel beyond the shores of the UK. There are family history societies which can advise and certainly research work should begin before travelling overseas. Ancestry and other sites should be first searched for archives for the relevant country which should provide some clues. Language skills should also be considered because, for example, German archives are likely to be written in German; some countries, depending on the age of the documents, may have material written in Latin. Some material for immigrants may be found in specialised repositories in the UK; there are a number of Polish research establishments in London which would be relevant for ancestors who travelled from Poland to the UK, but again expect the documents to be in Polish, or perhaps Yiddish if these were Polish Jews. While even UK county boundary changes can pose a problem, on the Continent there have been wholescale changes to national boundaries. Poland's boundaries have altered in the last century and the same goes for Germany and France, given the wars of the later nineteenth to mid-twentieth centuries. Damage by twentieth-century warfare has also depleted the pre-1945 archives of these countries. However, given that many ancestors moved to Australia, America and New Zealand, this is less of a problem given that these are all predominantly English-speaking countries whose boundaries have remained less inconstant. More importantly, these countries have not been affected by warfare within their borders in the twentieth century.

Chapter 10

ARCHIVES AND LIBRARIES

There are thousands of places in Britain where material for research can be located. By no means will a researcher need to go to many of these, for some material is available online. Even if it were not, only some of these would need to be visited, depending on both geography and subject matter. County and borough record offices whose remit covers where your ancestors lived are a must; others may need visiting depending on ancestors' occupation(s), religion and other attributes.

Boundary changes and location of records

Archives are usually to be found in the county or city where they were created. Thus a county record office will collect material based on geography. Yet there have been many boundary changes in the late nineteenth and twentieth centuries. In 1900 parishes in north-west Kent and north-east Surrey were incorporated into the county of London. In 1965 the counties of London and Middlesex were merged to form the new county of Greater London and at borough level, boroughs merged to become larger but fewer. Parts of Essex, Surrey and Kent and a little of southern Hertfordshire were also absorbed. Then in 1974, counties were merged, abolished and boundaries redrawn. The West Riding of Yorkshire was divided into West and South Yorkshire, with a few parishes being given to the new Greater Manchester and North Yorkshire. Cumberland, Westmorland and the Furness areas of Lancashire were merged to become Cumbria. Rutland was abolished. Humberside replaced the East Riding of Yorkshire and Avon replaced part of Somerset and districts adjacent. On a lesser level, some parishes on county borders became part of different counties. In the 1990s there were additional changes, bringing back counties that had been renamed or abolished (though not Middlesex). There have also been significant changes in Scotland and Wales with a reduction in counties (though in Wales these were increased in 1996) and their renaming in the twentieth century.

The issue for archives is that some archives are not in the county record office which is concurrent with the present county. Some institutions took archives prior to the introduction of county record offices. For example, the University of York's Borthwick Institute has many archives of parishes throughout the three ancient Ridings of Yorkshire, including the city of York. This was before the inception of the county record offices of these places who also hold parish archives for these counties. There is a similarly complex situation in Greater London. So the archives for a particular parish could be found in the London borough archives and the county record office for Greater London (The London Archives; TLA) and possibly even in the county record office for the former county. So for example, while researching Deptford, once in Kent, then a London borough (Deptford) in 1900, and then part of the London Borough of Lewisham in 1965, the author went to TLA, Lewisham Local Studies Centre (the borough archives) and the Kent History and Library Centre (in Maidstone).

The whereabouts of archives are best found by using TNA's Discovery site, which not only covers TNA's holdings but also those of other repositories in England and Wales. For

Scotland, a great many archives are at the National Records of Scotland in Princes' Street, Edinburgh, only about 10 minutes' walk from Waverley Railway Station. Most of Scotland's county record offices were created in relatively recent decades after the majority of the English record offices were founded. Hence many archives that would have gone to county record offices, were sent to the NRS. There is a website covering Scottish record offices hosted by the NRS and this should be a first port of call for Scottish archives.

Archives and libraries

Local archives are in the care of the unit of local government which administers the county or city borough in question. So these will be the county council in most cases, but could be the city archives as in the case of York, or the borough council in the case of Greater London and Greater Manchester boroughs. County record offices may have several branches; the West Yorkshire Archive Service has its headquarters in Wakefield but has branches in Leeds, Bradford, Halifax and Huddersfield. Or, as is the case in Cambridgeshire and Essex, there is one repository and that is in the county town: Cambridge and Chelmsford respectively. The staffing and funding of these services is very diverse; one London borough only has a part-time archivist and others have several members of staff, some qualified and some not.

Their core archive holdings are the records of their parent body and its predecessors. These will include the county quarter sessions and those of the county (or borough) council from 1889 and their predecessors. They will also include archives deposited or donated by private individuals and organisations. These could include deeds, diaries, correspondence of families and individuals, and documents created by clubs and societies, businesses, churches and so on. Although some of this material will date back to the Middle Ages, most will be from the nineteenth and twentieth

Essex Record Office. *(Ruth Smith, 2025)*

centuries. The collection policy is geographically based, so an archive will only collect material relevant to their district, though archives of estates are generally kept together so that one repository will have estate records which contain information about land in more than one county.

Information about archival holdings can be found by checking the appropriate website and exploring the online catalogue. An appointment should be made to view material in advance of a visit as space is often limited and material may be held in out stores as archives' on site storage capacity has usually been exceeded. Items can usually be ordered via the online catalogue.

Many archives are part of the ARA network (Archives and Record Association, the professional body of archivists and records managers) which require a reader's card to view material. This entails bringing proof of identity, but the card can be used in a number of archives. Not all require reader's cards; many of the London repositories do not, but many will need a reader to sign a visitors' book stipulating compliance to the rules of the place – pencils only to be used being a prime rule. Readers are usually allowed to take photographs of original documents but a fee will have to be paid; sometimes a flat daily fee, sometimes by number of photographs taken.

The readers' room where documents are viewed usually has relevant local history books on the shelves (useful for browsing when waiting for documents). Archives will be brought to the room and these are requested from the enquiry / issue desk and then can be collected by the reader who has ordered them.

Opening hours vary hugely, in part due to staffing levels; some have a single member of staff, and sometimes part-time. Some record offices have several branches (Norfolk has three) and so appointments must be made to avoid a wasted visit. Some county record offices are in the city or town centre in question, as in York, but some are a few miles from the city centre such as East Sussex Record Office which is on the far east side of Brighton, having moved from the county town of Lewes in the 2010s.

The National Archives

The National Archives was established as the Public Record Office in Chancery Lane in 1841, as the first public archive in Britain and so was a product of the Victorian era. Since the 1990s it has been wholly based at the site in Kew and was renamed in 2001. It is basically the archive office of the British government and its various departments. Records no longer in use for day-to-day purposes are sent here, but only about 5 per cent of paperwork created does so.

National Archives. *(Author photograph, 2025)*

The National Archives is on Ruskin Avenue. It is about ten minutes walk from the Kew Gardens underground station on the District line and about ten minutes walk from the nearest bus stop for the number 65 bus (on Kew Road). There is also a car park.

Two major departments of state which have already been mentioned which have created archives are the War Office and the Admiralty. There are also the archives of the Home Office, the Foreign and Colonial Offices and the Metropolitan Police (under the command of the Home Secretary until 2000). Other archives relevant to criminal ancestors are those of the department of the public prosecutor and the prison commission.

TNA has an open access library which includes many runs of annual publications, periodicals and other books relevant to British and overseas history. There are also copies of the Army List, the Navy List, Crockford's, Medical and Law listings, as well as a handful of county and city directories for example. Then there are the public terminals which can be viewed by anyone who visits; no appointment or reader's ticket is needed. These include access to FindMyPast and Ancestry.

However, most researchers who are serious about their history will want to view original paper documents, because only a minority of papers are available electronically. To do so, a reader's ticket is needed and this lasts two years. It can be easily renewed. It is free to obtain one, but you will need to present proof of identity such as a valid passport, driving licence, recent utility bills and so on. For new readers it is advisable to fill in as much of this on TNA's website in advance of your visit. This has the advantage of saving you time on arrival and letting you order up to twelve documents in advance of the visit.

Once there you will need to divest yourself of any coats and bags you have; there are free lockers and coat hangers on the ground floor, just past the shop and the exhibition room on the right. Be prepared to show any papers (preferably in a bound volume rather than loose) or laptops that you bring into the reading rooms to the attendants. Do not bring any food or drink – or worse, pens or erasers with you (pencils are allowed, minus eraser).

If you have ordered documents in advance, which you must do so at least a week before the day you propose to visit, you can tap your reader's card to obtain your seat number and this will also give you the location of your documents; on the first or second floor; for sensitive material, in the invigilation room. The seat number is also the number of the locker where your archives will be located – unless the items are in the smaller second-floor reading room, in which case you should go to the customer service point there and inform staff of your seat number and the document you want to see first.

If you do not book archives in advance, or once you have read through all those you have ordered, you can order archives using the computers on site. Up to three can be ordered and it can take up to an hour before they arrive. It is worth ordering items once your three have arrived so as to make the most efficient use of your time. Ordering usually ceases two hours before the time of closure, so usually at 3 pm, except for the days when there are evening openings (to 7 pm), Tuesday and Thursday.

Each floor also has a reader adviser to help resolve any specific research problems. Needless to say, conversation has to be kept to an absolute minimum and it is one of the few places in which mobile phone conversation is all but unknown.

One great advantage with TNA is that unlike other archives and libraries, electronic copying is free (reproduction of material in publications is another and expensive matter but this will be less of a problem, or none, to the family historian than to those writing for publication). This enables a researcher to photograph many documents for further investigation at leisure and so gives more time for research once at TNA, instead of having to decide whether to pay out in fees or scribble away at a fast rate of knots.

On the ground floor is the exhibition room, where there are displays of material and captions, a shop which sells many family history guides, including many from this series, as well as general military, criminal and other history books. There is also a café and place for readers to eat and talk.

At time of writing the reading rooms (and the book shop and exhibition) of TNA are open from 9.30–5 on Wednesday, Friday and Saturday, and from 9.30–7 on Tuesday and Thursday, with very occasional Sunday opening. Mondays are closed. Access to the building is allowed from 9 am which allows time to put items in lockers, use the toilets etc.

National Records of Scotland

Located at the east end of Princes Street in central Edinburgh and very close to the city's main railway station (Waverley) this is an imposing structure. It was founded in the late eighteenth century as a repository for archives and open to researchers since 1847. The historic search room is on the first floor. For those accustomed to TNA, it is very small and may appear old fashioned. Coats and bags must be put in lockers on the ground floor and there is a small shop. Unlike TNA, documents must be ordered in advance with at least three days' notice. Opening hours are currently 9–4 on weekdays only. There is a digital search room for the material which has been digitised. As always, proof of identity is needed in order to obtain a readers' ticket.

National Library of Wales

Founded in 1907 and located on the slope near to the main university college campus at Aberystwyth, two proofs of identity are needed to obtain a reader's ticket. Items must be ordered electronically and it is open six days a week. The collection includes newspapers, tithe maps (these can be seen on the online site) and estate archives of many places in Wales. It also has valuable holdings of the Welsh Anglican dioceses and of nonconformist archives, especially of the presbyterian Church of Wales.

Specialist archives and libraries

Apart from central and local government there is a host of other places which hold material relevant to family history research. Some are the record offices of organisations, whether business, charity or professional. Many are based at that organisation's headquarters (often in London, such as Lambeth Palace Library and the National Army Museum for example) and some are at museums or libraries. Cathedrals, universities and college libraries hold archival collections. Some of these will be the archives and material concerned with the history of the institution and those men and women who were associated with it in the past. They almost all need a prior appointment and proof of identity before access is granted.

The library of the Society of Genealogists is worth an especial mention. Founded in 1911 it is now based at 40 Wharf Road, London N1 7GS. It contains copies of many key family history resources from throughout Britain. As this is a private library membership is by payment. It has a large collection of pedigrees and family trees, transcripts of parish records, court records, poor law records and apprenticeship papers. They also run a series of talks on particular types of ancestors or particular research institutions, and there are courses aimed at varying levels of family historians from novices upwards, some of which may be relevant to your research.

The British Library

Located at 96 Euston Road and therefore very close to King's Cross railway station, this is the storehouse of the nation's books, though many are held at the Boston Spa campus in West Yorkshire. It also holds a great deal of archival material and other primary sources as well as published books and pamphlets (including many electoral registers). The archival collection is held in the British Library Manuscripts Room on the second floor. The collection can be searched online for people and places. Much of the collection is made up of the correspondence of the great and good, as well as collections by antiquarians.

The other major source held here is the newspaper collection. Once housed at Colindale in north London, since about 2013 it has been split between the library's depository at Boston Spa and the main site at St Pancras. Newspapers, hard copy and microfilm, can be viewed on the second floor of the St Pancras site and also at the Boston Spa site. Some national newspapers are on microfilm, such as *The Times, The News of the World* and *The Guardian,* which are in open access cabinets, but the bulk of newspapers have to be ordered in advance. Some of these newspapers are paper originals (these being delicate and fragile may not always be accessible if they are in need of conservation). There are plenty of microfilm readers in this room. Anyone unfamiliar with this twentieth-century technology can ask a member of staff to help. Unfortunately a cyber attack in 2023 has led to the impossibility of sending anything seen on microfilm to your email address (still the case at the time of writing) and has prevented access to the British Newspaper archive on the British Library computers but it still can be accessed for free on researchers own device(s).

Access is by reader's ticket only. These can be had for free on proof of identity and last for two years. At the moment up to ten items can be ordered each day. The items held on site, which are the manuscripts and some of the newspapers, can be had after seventy minutes, but much material is held off site and at least forty-eight hours notice is needed to see these. All these can be ordered in advance by the British Library's website. The library is open six days a week, including three evenings. There are lockers in the basement where coats and bags must be deposited.

The Guildhall Library, Aldermanbury

This is the library of the corporation of the City of London and so its holdings are particularly rich in books about London and Londoners. But it also has an enormous collection of directories from all over the UK. Originals are produced though a few for London can be seen on microfilm. These have to be ordered in advance after searching the online catalogue. Entry to the library does not need a reader's ticket or proof of identity. It is open five days a week from 10–5. The nearby Bishopsgate Institute also holds a considerable collection of directories.

Cathedral archives

Many of the medieval Anglican cathedrals have their own archives/library where their archives are accessible. The Dean and Chapter is the administrative body which runs the cathedral, its staff and its property and archives usually date from the Middle Ages. Act books and minutes detail cathedral business and so if your ancestor was a canon or other member of cathedral staff they should be noted here. The Chapter Clerk's office correspondence may also be relevant. Preachers at the cathedral are listed in rotas. Dioceses employ many other people, not just clergymen and so there may be records of their employments. They also own much land which has accrued over the centuries and again, these leave records which have been kept.

University archives

Universities hold material about former staff and students, either centrally in their university archives and in collegiate universities, within the college libraries themselves. They may also hold other archives, especially relating to land and property owned by the university/college; this is often the case with the older colleges of the older universities as they were bequeathed to them. Former students and staff may have left their papers to their university. Access is easier for former students, but bona fide researchers can usually be granted access by prior application for a temporary ticket which may or may not be free.

New Bodleian Library, Oxford. *(Author photograph, 2025)*

Business archives

Businesses which still exist keep the records of their own organisation and these should include staff records if they have not been deposited elsewhere. These, of course, are private archives and there may or may not be a designated archivist employed there. Some City of London livery companies employ a part time archivist and retain their archives, though some have chosen to deposit them at the appropriate record office.

Archives of stately homes

Some archives of landowners have been deposited in record offices, such as the Temple Newsam and Nostell Priory papers which are at the Leeds branch of the West Yorkshire Archive Service, and many Scottish estate papers are at the National Records of Scotland. Other archives that are held privately are those of landowning families. These include those of the Duke of Devonshire, held at Chatsworth House in Derbyshire. At the latter, though entrance is now free to use the archives, booking must be made at least two weeks in advance and days of opening are Monday-Wednesday from 9.30–4.30 with an hour closure for lunch. The archive includes family and estate papers. There is also a freely available online database of about 4,500 people who have been employed on the estate in the past. Other stately homes with similar collections include the Salisbury home, Hatfield House in Hertfordshire, that of the Duke of Norfolk at Arundel Castle and that of the Bedford estates at Woburn Abbey.

Chapter 11

ONLINE RESOURCES

Although the majority of archives and local history sources remain undigitised, there has been a priority given for digtisation to those which have a clear genealogical use because that is where the bulk of the demand is. As time goes by more and more material is becoming accessible online, usually for a fee. Yet the convenience of being able to undertake research at home is a great boon and overcomes the restrictions of limited opening hours and time/cost of travel especially for those in employment or with other demands on their time. Some record offices and libraries offer these online resources for free on site. The online British Newspaper Archive can be viewed freely at the British Library (although currently only on the reader's own device because the BL's computers are still hors de combat following a cyber attack in 2023) and through local library services subscriptions, for example and TNA offers free access to FindMyPast; humbler places, such as Hillingdon Libraries often offer only Ancestry. The advantage of online access to the researcher is surely obvious in that it allows searches to be made and results to be found very quickly indeed; brief references to an ancestor can be found in seconds when searching manually would take days or weeks.

Newspapers

The Victorian era saw a huge increase of newspapers and especially in the mass market popular press with its emphasis on pictures and human interest stories aimed at the newly literate working class; 'written by office boys for office boys' was a famous comment on the *Daily Mail* founded in 1895. From 1853 to 1867 the number of newspapers published in Yorkshire rose from twenty to eighty-six.

The Times digital archive which initially covered 1785–1985 was the first newspaper to be available online; *The Manchester Guardian* from 1821 followed soon afterwards. But from about 2012 the British Newspaper Archive became the predominant online source for newspapers. It covers the years from 1700 (a great shame for this author when researching the later seventeenth century) to date. It includes hundreds of national and local newspapers. However, it does not cover every single newspaper title or edition (there are none for Southall between 1941 and 1974 for instance), and for many newspapers there are incomplete runs of what is covered in the nominal date range. Even within the apparent year range the coverage may be patchy. In some cases it will still be necessary to view the original newspaper or, more likely, a microfilmed version of it.

The site is searched by keyword but searches can be narrowed down considerably by a variety of techniques. First is by date, because searches can be made for an exact date range, for example, 1 March 1867 to 23 April 1868, or whatever date range you wish to employ. Second, they can be limited by newspaper. So if your ancestor lived in the environs of Keighley, West Yorkshire, restricting searches to *The Keighley News* would seem logical. Of course for some places, such as Brighton, there are a number of newspapers which cover the date range and so a search by each of these may be necessary. It is worth noting that 'local newspapers' were not entirely as parochial as some became in the twentieth century, but often included items of news from the other side of the country or overseas.

You might also want to consider using the 'Exact phrase' search box rather than the 'Keyword search' which will reduce the number of matches. Of course if the name you are searching for is relatively uncommon, such as Novissimo, this will not be an issue, but if the surname is Collins or Robinson it will be. Bear in mind that in the nineteenth century people were often referred to in the press by their surname, title and initials, rather than their Christian name.

Another thing worth pointing out is that the text of these newspapers has been digitised using Optical Character Recognition. This works well when the print of the original newspaper is clear and uniform but not so well, or even hopelessly, when the print is unclear, not straight or the delineation between columns is indistinct. The result is words which are misspelt, sometimes beyond recognition, and consequently not findable using a keyword search. Early newspapers (some certainly up to 1820 often printed the old 'long s' (ſ) (this is Unicode 017F) and annoyingly, the OCR program has not had this in its font, so regularly turns it into an 'f'. For example, this means that to search for the surnames Ross or Stevenson in these early papers you also need to try Rofs and Stevenfon. There are many cases of gibberish, but if you do a search for 'Thomas Ballyman Churley' you should find the *Exeter Flying Post* of 29 April 1830 where 'Mr Sweetland's' appears as 'Mr. SweetIlani!'Mi' and 'Mr. Sweeiland's', and 'of Thursday' appears as 'ot hbursdlay'. But if you limit a search to, say, 1830–1840, and search any term you'll see many entries with gobbledegook text, which proves the point that many keyword searches may fail unless the keyword happens to occur several times and at least one of them is right.

The site's index can be searched free of charge but if you want to read any of the articles thrown up by your search, you will need to pay (about 10 per cent of entries can be viewed for free). This can be done either by the month or annually. The latter works out least expensive pro rata. It depends how much use you think you will make of it. It has to be said that it can be highly addictive as it opens up all sorts of search opportunities and is being constantly updated with more newspapers, and also the extension of the date ranges of the existing newspapers. It is possible to search for additions to the site by searching for newly available material after a particular date of your choice. But it may be that your ancestors only make brief appearances in the press and so a month's intense use of it may be most cost effective.

It is worth noting that names in newspapers are not necessarily what we might expect. And keyword searches are literally what is typed in. Until well into the twentieth century people were often not known by their Christian names in text, hence Mr. J. Smith not John Smith or for women Mrs/Miss Jones not Martha Jones.

The other point is that there is a list of newspapers in the site, which are listed in alphabetical order and are given year ranges for what is on the site. This is not entirely reliable because in some cases there are gaps in these date ranges, though this might be rectified as time goes by and the site becomes more comprehensive.

There are other newspaper archives online. Much of what has been said above applies here, too. The Welsh newspapers site (https://newspapers.library.wales) covers 1804–1918 (mostly from 1880) and of course includes news stories from England and elsewhere. Several newspapers from Wales are included in this and all can be searched at once or individually by newspaper and by date and keyword. It can also be narrowed down by searching only 'Family Notices' or 'News' and by searching English language or Welsh language newspapers. At time of writing this is free to use. I found it by accident when researching an English family living in Kidwelly, Carmarthenshire, from 1898–1921 and it was very useful in learning about the involvement of the family in local sporting, political and religious events.

There is also the Trove site (https://trove.nla.gov.au/newspaper/) for Australian newspapers from at least 1848 and this is not only of relevance if your ancestors went to Australia, either voluntarily or were transported there. The newspapers here also have stories about Britain and not surprisingly, because most of the white settlers in Australia in the nineteenth century were of British stock and so would be interested in news back home. Searches can be limited by place, date and newspaper title. It is also free to use.

Manchester Library users, who do not have to live there but need to sign up for reader membership, can have free online access to *The Manchester Guardian*, a leading liberal newspaper of the Victorian period, covering 1821–2000 (in 1959 it moved to London and became *The Guardian*). Although the focus was on Manchester and Lancashire news, national news was also featured. The same institution also offers *The Times* online from 1785–2006.

The London Gazette can be viewed for free online (https://www.thegazette.co.uk). It was founded in 1665 as *The Oxford Gazette* and is the organ of official notices by the government so is not the place for exciting stories. It does, however, list official appointments in the armed forces and civil service as well as listing bankrupts. The box 'Search the archives' is the first step to search the site. The named individual may be mentioned many many times, but then the search can be updated by inserting a date range to and from and then a more manageable number of possibilities will be given.

Directories

The main source for historical directories from 1760–1914 is the Leicester University site, which is currently https://

le.ac.uk/libraries/special-collections/explore/historical-directories

It can be searched by historic county and then by date of directory. The pages can be read through or a keyword search can be made. The latter is perhaps less useful because it will bring a large number of hits. There are over 600 directories here and so it is a very useful source. However, these are a minority of what actually exists and so it may still be necessary to consult paper directories.

Ancestry is a leading, perhaps *the* leading online family history source. It is unlikely that any researcher into family history can do without it, as well as other researchers who are working on any historical subject. It is particularly rich for sources for the Victorian era (the census, civil registration and wills after 1858 being the most useful ones).

The obvious search method is the general one in which the name of the person, place associated with them and year of birth is typed in. This should bring up a crop of probably relevant records which in turn will suggest others. However, it is also possible to search individual databases. A number of generic ones, such as births, marriages and deaths, military, census collections, wills are given, but so is a search Card Catalogue option. This allows a search by keyword for a subject (not a personal name), so typing in Medical would bring up the Medical Register, The Medical Directory etc. A large number of databases will be listed and can be reduced by country – and Ancestry has much more about the USA and UK than any other country. Then these can be searched if you think you have a doctor ancestor. Unfortunately there is no directory of domestic servants, agricultural labourers or factory workers! But there are ones for railway workers and engineers. FindMyPast is another important genealogical tool and it has a great deal of overlap with Ancestry. However, it has much more besides.

The *Oxford Dictionary of National Biography* (ODNB) is perhaps an overlooked source. Published in 2004 it supersedes the late nineteenth century *Dictionary of National Biography* (which can be viewed on Ancestry). It focuses on providing the biographies of about 60,000 historically important Britons and for the Victorians they include the infamous as well as the socially prestigious. This is, of course, only a very small minority of the population. However, it can be searched online, not only by the subject of each biography but by a search of the text for any individual who might be mentioned in the articles of the great and not so good. Many libraries have subscriptions to the ODNB so library card holders can search it freely at their nearest library – and in some cases remotely too, Ealing allows this, https://libraries.ealing.gov.uk/digital-content/digital-library/dictionaries-guides-and-references, click on the link, select Institution, Ealing etc, then enter library card number prefixed by EAL. This webpage used to point this out for the three Oxford sources when I originally wrote the text of it, but now it doesn't, so no one would ever know or be able to guess!

TNA has Discovery, which is a tool for searching the whereabouts of archives not only held by itself, but to others held throughout England; likewise, the NRS has a similar database covering some other Scottish archives. Discovery can restrict searches by TNA or other archives or both, and then searches can be further narrowed down. In the case of TNA's holdings this can be by date ranges (pre-determined by the site not the researcher) and/or by department (e.g., Home Office, War Office, Admiralty etc.).

Some of these searches will bring up archives of direct significance for an individual, for example a military or police record. So a search of William Ogden brings up the will of the same, a gentleman of Kentish Town, proved in

1850 (TNA reference: PROB11/2101/287). But others will not be as useful and merely give the name of a document, e.g., register of freemen of the city of Norwich for 1868 is simply given as N/T314/7 and will have to be seen at the county archives and which may or may not list your Norwich ancestor.

Findagrave (https://www.findagrave.com) is another useful source. This is an international index to graves from a great many cemeteries worldwide. Details provided after a name search can vary considerably but can include dates and places of birth and death, cemetery and plot number and perhaps a picture. The wording on the stone or memorial may also be found here. It is a site to which the public contributes and so perhaps there is an emphasis on the famous and notorious. It can be searched by cemetery or churchyard if these are known to you. It is not, of course, comprehensive and so a negative search is not absolutely definitive. A search on the list of cemeteries will be useful here to ascertain if the cemetery in question is not listed, though the parishes are listed as the modern district council names. An example from Scarborough churchyard is as follows:

HERE
LIE THE REMAINS OF
ANNE BRONTE
DAUGHTER OF THE
Revd. P. BRONTE
Incumbent of Haworth, Yorkshire
She died Aged 28
MAY 28th 1849

Now, this is not likely to bring your researches much forward because date of death, age and father's name can be easily ascertained from other sources such as burial registers, death certificates and census returns. However, it is good to see the physical remains associated with our ancestors and to take photographs of such or if the image is online to copy it. Furthermore if the name is a relatively common one, other information on a grave, such as spouse or children, might clarify that this is the right grave.

Wills from 1858 can be searched for and ordered on the British government's website (https://www.gov.uk/search-wills-probate). You will need to know the name and year of death to search. Then it can be further narrowed down by a keyword, month and day of death and of probate. The appropriate page of the index book should appear and one example is as follows:

> GREENWOOD, William
> Estate under £450
> 6 August. The Will of William Greenwood, late of Crossley-terrace in the County of York, weaver who died 31 July 1877 at Halifax was proved at the Principal Registry by Thomas Greenwood of 2 Ely Davys Road Croydon in the county of Surrey Cabinet maker the son and Ann Crabtree (wife of John Crabtree) of Crossley-terrace, the daughter the Executors

Some of these details then need to be completed on the outline form; name, dates of death and probate and the registry where the will was proved. It is necessary to sign up to the site and pay the fee (£1.50 at time of writing) and then wait a week or so to have notification of the will which must then be downloaded.

Record Societies

Since the nineteenth century there have been many record societies in Britain which have published an annual volume, a transcription of a set of archives about a particular topic or individual, making such information more easily accessible and each volume is indexed by name and place. In more recent years many of these have been made available online for free. Most English counties have a record society, and there is a Scottish record society as well as others devoted to particular subjects. They cover all eras from the archaeological and medieval to the twentieth century. Some cover the Victorian era; the Lancashire and Cheshire Record Society have a volume of Lancashire wills from 1838 to 1858, the family papers of Benjamin Shaw of Dent, Dolphinhome and Preston from 1774 to 1841 and the diary of John O'Neill, a weaver, from 1856 to 1875. It is an easy task to search the internet to find the record society/ies which cover the county/ies that your ancestors lived in and check whether such material might be relevant.

Family History societies are mostly geographically based by county or even by town or city. They each have websites in which some material relevant to the county is to be found. Most have members' pages which give more information and usually a subscription fee will allow access to these.

There are doubtless many other online sources, and there will be many more in the forthcoming years. Existing websites will probably be expanded and more resources will be added to them. For instance Ancestry is constantly being added to and the British Newspaper Archive likewise, so it is always worth returning to sites after the initial trawl. New sources on the same site may well be highlighted.

Online resources are very important for research and provide shortcuts that were impossible for researchers in the 1990s and earlier. They provide the opportunity for speculative searches that would otherwise be very time consuming and might throw up additional information.

However, by themselves they will take a researcher only so far. There are many sources only available in paper format, which will need to be searched if the researcher is to find as much as they can. Both source types are needed and go hand in hand.

Chapter 12

SPORT AND LEISURE

The Victorian working man had far more hours of labour than his modern counterpart. Hours were long, but as the century progressed they were reduced and half days on Saturdays became the norm. Even so, working weeks of fifty hours or more were common. In 1871 Bank holidays were introduced. However, leisure pursuits existed, were expanded and became more organised in the Victorian era. The English Football League was inaugurated in 1888. There were also intellectual pursuits and youth movements by the end of the century. Political participation was another facet of leisure time, doubtless allied to the increase in the electorate, but earlier there were pressure group movements on a national scale. These groups were mostly male dominated and often exclusively male, but some had female members and some were exclusively female, especially those for some sports.

Very few of these records have been digitised; on Ancestry there is a database of English cricketers from 1845 onwards only; apart from date and place of birth of the named cricketer, there is only his designation as a batsman. FindMyPast has the records of two cricket clubs on its pages.

Many clubs and societies do not have records going back to when the club began. Often records of the early days were not kept and it was only when activities became formalised

Mr A.J. Webbe, Middlesex cricketer. *(Author's copy of* The Strand, *1893)*

and a committee appointed that their actions were recorded on paper. This is often the case with sports clubs rather than more intellectual and academic pastimes. This can lead to uncertainty as to when a club was formed and who the founders were.

Clubs were as much about social events as about the matter that they purportedly pursued. There were concerts, dinners, dances and excursions to which non-members – often female – were invited (in the case of male clubs; the reverse applied for female clubs). The variety of home entertainments now known in the twenty-first century did not then exist; even the wireless had to wait until the twentieth century. Homes were not in other ways as attractive as they would be in later decades and so the impulse to spend leisure time with men of similar interests and outlooks was stronger than now.

Sports

As well as the foundation of the football league and rugby league in this period, both of which were highly popular and facilitated by the growth of the railway network, there were many local groups that sprang up for swimming, bowls, tennis, badminton and cycling, as well as for cricket, football and rugby. Many were for men, but there were some women's groups as well. There was an Ealing Ladies Hockey Club from 1888.

Minute books of clubs and societies often survive and these are useful sources; the more involved a member, the greater the information about them. There may be membership lists and club fixture cards. The latter were produced at the beginning of every annual sports season and were given to each member. They list the inter-club matches and the individual club competitions. They might also list all club members and the rules of the club, such as what the annual subscriptions were and what the club uniform consisted of. If the club survived for decades there may be a published history of the club. Local newspapers covered local sports matches and their attendant social activities. Usually accounts of matches and team members (usually only known by surname and initial(s)) who played were published, so for cricket matches you can see how many runs each gained; there may even be comments about

Shooting Club. *(Author's copy of* The Strand, *1893)*

the prowess of individual players. Minute books are also useful for those members who were on the club's committee as they will be mentioned as attending meetings and are usually noted at the start of the record of each meeting, and for specific actions as noted in the main text of the minutes.

Annual reports were printed and are another good source for the club's history and its members.

Politics

Political involvement was far greater in this period than any other and it was not confined to voting in or out governments every few years. Political parties aimed to create mass membership in order to support their cause at election times, but there was more to it than this. Election meetings were popular events to go to and crowds came out in the streets to hear the results being announced. Victorian politics was dominated by the Liberal and Conservative parties, who had emerged from the Whigs and the Tories of the eighteenth century. In 1893 there was the fledging Independent Labour Party, though its day was yet to come. *The Labour Annual* began publication in 1895 and it listed prominent figures in the labour movement, especially leading trades unionists and left wing writers. Some copies of this can be found at the Institute of Historical Research in London.

The National Union of Conservative and Unionist Associations' archives from 1867 are to be found at the Bodleian Library, Oxford, as part of the Conservative Party archives there. Material from the regional offices from 1886 and from the national conferences from 1867 can be seen there. One prominent group was the Primrose League, founded in memory of Benjamin Disraeli, once Conservative Prime Minister, in 1883. This was predominantly made up of working-class Conservatives and there were branches throughout the country. Often records exist for only a few years of each branch's existence; in the case of the Lostwithiel branch in Cornwall, this is only a membership register for 1888–92. At Staffordshire Record Office are subscription books from 1888 to 1922, listing local Liberal party members and the sums they promised for party work, and lists of candidates for membership with those who proposed them from 1892 to 1905, and these give an indication of relationships to other party members.

There were also major single-issue pressure groups which existed for a limited period of time in the early Victorian era. Some were predominantly middle class. One was the Anti-Corn Law League, which became a national body in 1838 and lobbied to have the Corn Laws abolished (occurring in 1846). There was the British and Foreign Anti-Slavery Society, established in London in 1839, who wanted to see slavery stamped out globally after the British abolition, and the more working-class Chartists, who sought parliamentary reform from 1838 to 1857. Although these bodies were national, they had many local branches in towns and cities.

Other clubs and societies

There had been intellectual and philosophical societies in the eighteenth century catering for gentlemen in the towns and cities as discussion groups. Many more such societies were founded in the Victorian era. The study of history, archaeology and the natural world were some of the favourite topics and there were regular meetings, which were often lectures and discussion groups and excursions, as well as an annual journal to record the year's activities and advertise future events.

These journals are a prime source for the family historian because they often list members and their addresses. There are usually articles by members and references to other work or activities by some. There may also be additional material such as minute books. Clubs and societies often had their excursions, meetings and social events reported in the local press. Clubs were male dominated but some did allow female members. Prominent club members, especially those on the committee, will be mentioned more than any other.

As ever with any organisation, those who are prominent in running it will tend to feature more in the records than those who are not. So the people who attend committee meetings will be recorded in minute books, as is the case with the Acton Literary Club for 1887–1890. These minute books also feature the programmes for social events. It seems that the Acton Literary Club as was not uncommon at the time, and had musical evenings which women as well as men attended. Programmes for these evenings have been stuck into the said minute book and these list the club members who were performing songs either as solos or as a duet with a female singer.

Journals of such societies often record the club's activities for the past year and even provide summaries of the lectures given. Certainly this is the case with the Ealing Microscopical and Natural History Society. Excursions are also recorded and those leading them or taking a prominent role in arranging them should be noted.

Temperance was a social concern among many, especially churches, in order to combat the evils of alcohol. Temperance societies were formed and coffee taverns established, often in alliance with local churches. In 1886 the Ealing branch of the Sons of Temperance was formed. The membership book was signed by those who could 'hereby pledge myself that I shall not make, buy, sell or use as a beverage, any spirituous or malt liquors, wine or cider'. There followed a list of people, giving the date pledged, their name, age on last birthday, address and occupation. The final column was cause of leaving, if any. Often this was because they had left the district. One example was that of Edward Joshua Wall, who signed up on 21 February 1886, aged 28, of Western Road, Ealing, an accountant. He was 'expelled for non payment of subscription'.

There were also rather more exclusive social clubs which sprang into being in this period; many based in London, especially around Pall Mall (Sherlock Holmes fans will recall Mycroft Holmes being a member of the misanthropic – and fictional – Diogenes Club). Some of these catered for specific groups, such as university men or army and naval officers (the United Service Club was for senior officers – records are at the National Army Museum), as well as the great political clubs such as the Carlton (Conservatives) and the Reform (Liberals). The Travellers' Club included many civil servants, diplomats and soldiers among its members. Some of these clubs are now defunct, but many still exist and so it would be worth contacting them about any relevant archival material.

The Royal Society of Arts, catering for authors, artists and sculptors, had some of its membership details available on FindMyPast. They give the member's name and address, the proposer, date of membership and fee. William Davy of 17 Gate Drive, Lincoln Inn's Fields, was one such member. He was proposed by one J.B. Cundall and was elected on 26 January 1878. He had to pay £2 2s by Christmas. It was not only in London that such clubs existed. In Edinburgh there was the Buchanan Society existing from 1725–1848 for members of the clan Buchanan. The listings are especially useful because they list not only individuals, but also refer to other family members who were club members too. Andrew Buchanan, tobacconist and member since 1842, was a son of John, a horse setter of Glasgow and a member from 1814. He also had brothers in the same club.

Youth

Towards the end of our period several youth organisations were formed which became national and even international in scope. The first was the Boys' Brigade, founded in Glasgow in 1883. In 1891 there was the Church Lads' Brigade. These were Christian groups for young people (initially only boys) which became national bodies in the late Victorian era. They were inter-denominational, but some denominational and even Jewish groups were formed. Archives are usually found in county record offices but many are held privately. Records include membership lists and photographs, as well as the minutes and other more general records.

You may already know that your Victorian ancestor played cricket for a local or works' team, but even if you have no idea what his leisure activities were, it is worth seeing what clubs and societies were in the locality in which they lived and then see whether they have left any surviving records. Sometimes the early records do not survive, but sometimes they do. Even if that is not the case, the local newspaper will certainly have recorded the clubs' activities in their columns and so there might be a reference there. Sporting events are often covered in the press, as are social events. Of course many people's leisure activities are passive: going to the pub, to a sports match or a music hall or theatre, and of these there is unlikely to be much record unless someone made a personal note of it, or there was an untoward incident involving them which led to it being reported.

Greenwich Park. *(Author's postcard)*

CONCLUSION

Compared to earlier periods in history the Victorian age offers a treasure trove of sources for the family historian. It is not only the well known sources of civil registration certificates and census returns, but far more, as has been outlined in this book. To an extent, chance will play its part; some ancestors will make a greater impact on the existing records than others.

It is important to work backwards from 1901 carefully and not make an instant leap to 1837. The period is a manageable chunk of family history – sixty-four years – and is an important stepping stone to earlier centuries, so it is necessary to be as correct as possible with Victorian ancestors as they are the link with more bygone years.

There may be problems. These should not be seen as absolute stumbling blocks but only a call maybe to check other family members and see how you proceed with them. As said, some may be easier to trace than others and luck will play a part. Newly digitised records may provide a clue so it is always worth going back to a source, as new material is constantly being added and that might help.

Recently I was looking into the life of John Starchfield, a working-class man born into an impoverished background in north London in the later nineteenth century. His army record gave varying dates for his birth and these did not always accord with his census returns or death certificate. He did not seem to have been baptised nor could a birth certificate be found. I was resolved to live with this uncertainty and the fact that his parents did not bother to register his birth. Then on reading an early twentieth-century memoir which referred to him I found that his real surname was Sarsfield. With this new name to search I quickly found his birth certificate and that added a new element to his story.

So, start with what you know from the census returns and civil registration certificates. These will provide names, ages, occupations, localities and other family members. These can then be traced by investigating these different clues. There can also be 'blanket' searches using the major websites such as Ancestry.co.uk and FindMyPast and the British Newspaper Archive. With the latter, if you do find someone of the correct name, you need to check this against other known information such as occupation, address, age and so forth to ensure it is the right person. This may not be possible, so mark them with a question mark and do additional work.

When researching it is important to note what you have looked at and where information comes from. This is the case even if it is a negative result, so as to avoid wasting time in the future. With digital sources, mark when you looked at the source, as this will assist if you revisit it as searches can often be made on material added after a chosen date.

Well, if you have reached this far, there is no need for the author to say anything more than to wish every reader researching their Victorian ancestors good luck on their researches.

BIBLIOGRAPHY

Crail, Mark, *Tracing your Labour Movement Ancestors* (Pen and Sword Books Ltd., 2020)

Fowler, Simon, *Tracing your Army Ancestors* (Pen and Sword Books Ltd., 2017)

Fowler, Simon, *Tracing your Naval Ancestors* (Pen and Sword Books Ltd., 2012)

Higgs, Michelle, *Tracing your Servant Ancestors* (Pen and Sword Books Ltd., 2020)

Jolly, Emma, *Tracing your British Indian Ancestors* (Pen and Sword Books Ltd., 2012)

Wenzerul, Rosemary, *Tracing your Jewish Ancestors* (Pen and Sword Books Ltd., 2015)

Wilkes, Sue, *Tracing your Canal Ancestors* (Pen and Sword Books Ltd., 2012)

INDEX